Birds

of the World
BY LESTER L. SHORT

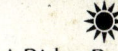

A Ridge Press Book

Bantam Books
Toronto • New York • London

Photo Credits

AR—Ardea
BC—Bruce Coleman
CL—Cornell Laboratory
    of Ornithology
LR—Luisa Ricciarini
M—Mauritius
NA—National Audubon Society
OS—Östman Agency
PM—Pictor Milano
PR—Photo Researchers

F. J. Alsop III (BC): 156; A. W. Ambler (NA): 82 (rt.), 113; American Museum of Natural History: 7, 40, 93, 97, 98, 124; Ron Austing (BC): 148; Jen & Des Bartlett (BC): 23, 118, 145 (btm. rt.), 154; Erwin A. Bauer: 26, 29 (top); Alouise Boker (NA): 145 (top); H. Brown (CL): 153 (top); J. Brownlie (BC): 49; Giuliano Cappelli (LR): 35, 61; E. G. Carle (PM): 75; Bruce Coleman (BC): 37, 50, 53 (btm. rt.), 57, 66, 89, 126, 140 (rt.), 143; Crader (M): 22; Werner Curth (M): 117; Thase Daniel: 99, (BC): 106, 122; A. J. Deane (BC): 62, 78, 91; H. D. deBruin (PM): 51; John S. Dunning (AR): 94, 101, (CL): 151, 155, (PR): 103; M. D. England (AR): 86; F. Erize (BC): 18; Kenneth W. Fink (BC): 53 (top rt. & btm. left), 85, 138, (NA): 8; Michael Freeman (BC): 79 (rt.); Freytag (M): 38; Michael Gochfeld: 109; T. W. Hall (BC): 67; Mike Hopiak: 80 (top rt.), 95, 104, 149; E. Hosking (BC): 74, 114; D. Hughes (BC): 32; E. Hummel (PM): 34; P. Johnson (OS): 9 (left); Michael Kleinbaum: 28; Marilyn Krog: 5 (left), 73, 87, 88, 96, 147, 153 (btm.); Frank W. Lane (BC): 128 (rt.); Cyril Laubscher (BC): 128 (left), 137, 145 (btm. left); Eric Lindgren (AR): 21 (top), 92; Aldo Margiocco: 30, 43, 44, 58, 112; J. Markham (BC): 131; Giuseppe Mazza: 19, 33, 39, 42, 47, 59, 125; Jeremy McCabe (BC): 135; E. McNamara (AR): 127; J. F. Millies (PM): 64; Mohn (PM): 80 (btm.); P. Morris (AR): 21 (btm.); Werner H. Muller (PM): 20, 141; Nico Myburgh (BC): 134; Norman Myers (BC): 31; G. Nystrand (BC): 53 (top); F. Park (PM): 110, 136; Graham Pizzey (PR): 140 (left); Hans Reinhard (BC): 70, 115, (M): 36, 146, (PM): 9 (rt.), 46, 116; L. L. T. Rhodes: 69; H. Rivarola (BC): 14, 108; Alan Root (BC): 79 (left); Angelo P. Rossi: 41, 68, 71, 72, 76, 90, 100, 105, 111, 120, 121; Leonard Lee Rue III: 54, 83; Schmidecker (M): 45; Walter Schmidt (PM): 142; Heinz Schrempp/F.L. (BC): 123, (M): 129, 132; Paul Schwartz (PR): 102; V. Serventy (BC): 65; Peter Slater (PR): 130 (top), 139; Michael C. J. Smith (NA): 25 (left); Philip M. Smith (BC): 25 (rt.); M. F. Soper (BC): 27, 29 (btm.); Lynn M. Stone (NA): 55; Marty Stouffer (BC): 48, 56; W. R. Taylor (AR): 130 (btm.), 133; Charles Van Riper: 150; Joseph VanWormer (BC): 5 (rt.), 77, (BC): 63, 107, 119; R. T. W. (OS): 157; J. Wallis (BC): 82 (left); Gary R. Zahm (BC): 80 (top left); D. Zingel (BC): 24, (PM): 60; Frank Zingel/F.L. (BC): 84

Front Cover: Great Horned Owl, J. H. Carmichael, Jr. (BC); Back Cover:
Steppe Eagle, Norman Myers (BC); Title Page: top left, Hen Harrier, Eric Soothill (BC);
btm. left, Nightingales, Hans Reinhard (BC); right, Aracari, S. C. Bisserot (BC)
Drawings: Denis Prince

BIRDS OF THE WORLD

A Bantam Book published by arrangement with The Ridge Press, Inc.
Text prepared under the supervision of Laurence Urdang Inc.
Designed and produced by The Ridge Press, Inc. All rights reserved.
Copyright 1975 in all countries of the International Copyright Union by
The Ridge Press, Inc. This book may not be reproduced in whole
or in part by mimeograph or any other means, without permission.
For information address: The Ridge Press, Inc.,
25 West 43rd Street, New York, N.Y. 10036.
Library of Congress Catalog Card Number: 75-10947
Published simultaneously in the United States and Canada.

Bantam Books are published by Bantam Books, Inc.
Its trademark, consisting of the words "Bantam Books" and the portrayal
of a bantam, is registered in the United States Patent Office
and in other countries. Marca Registrada.
Bantam Books, Inc., 666 Fifth Avenue, New York, N.Y. 10019.
Printed in Italy by Mondadori Editore, Verona.

Contents

- 5 Introduction
- 18 Crested Tinamou
- 19 Ostrich
- 20 Common Rhea
- 21 Emu
- 22 Kiwi
- 23 Red-throated Loon
- 24 Great Crested Grebe
- 25 Emperor Penguin
- 26 Laysan Albatross
- 27 Sooty Shearwater
- 28 Wilson's Petrel
- 29 Red-tailed Tropicbird
- 30 Red-footed Booby
- 31 Great Cormorant
- 32 Anhinga
- 33 White Pelican
- 34 Magnificent Frigatebird
- 35 Black Swan
- 36 Mallard
- 37 Smew
- 38 Greater Flamingo
- 39 Cattle Egret
- 40 Shoebill Stork
- 41 Scarlet Ibis
- 42 Saddlebill Stork
- 43 Andean Condor
- 44 Osprey
- 45 Lammergeyer
- 46 Northern Goshawk
- 47 Secretarybird
- 48 Peregrine Falcon
- 49 Mallee Fowl
- 50 Great Curassow
- 51 Helmeted Guineafowl
- 52 Black Grouse
- 52 Lady Amherst Pheasant
- 54 Turkey
- 55 Limpkin
- 56 Clapper Rail
- 57 Sunbittern
- 58 Sarus Crane
- 59 Great Bustard
- 60 Common Oystercatcher
- 61 Avocet
- 62 Pratincole
- 63 Killdeer
- 64 Dunlin
- 65 Silver Gull
- 66 Inca Tern
- 67 Tufted Puffin
- 68 Pintailed Sandgrouse
- 69 Victoria Crested Pigeon
- 70 Wood Pigeon
- 71 Thick-billed Green Pigeon
- 72 Kea
- 73 Rainbow Lorikeet
- 74 Monk Parakeet
- 75 Scarlet Macaw
- 76 White-crested Touraco
- 77 Common Roadrunner
- 78 Klaas' Cuckoo
- 79 Hoatzin
- 81 Burrowing Owl
- 81 Snowy Owl
- 82 Tawny Frogmouth
- 83 Whip-poor-will
- 84 Swift
- 85 Costa's Hummingbird
- 86 Streamertail
- 87 Long-tailed Sylph
- 88 Red-faced Mousebird
- 89 Quetzal

90	Black-capped Kingfisher	125	Marsh Warbler
91	Carmine Bee-eater	126	Firecrest
92	Dollarbird	127	Variegated Blue-wren
93	Southern Ground Hornbill	128	Paradise Flycatcher
94	Chestnut-capped Puffbird	129	Pied Flycatcher
95	Gaudy Barbet	130	Red-capped Robin
96	Collared Aracari	131	Nuthatch
97	Rufous Piculet	132	Great Tit
98	Andean Flicker	133	Mistletoebird
99	Red-cockaded Woodpecker	134	Malachite Sunbird
100	Hornero	135	Oriental White-eye
101	Red-billed Scythebill	136	Red Wattlebird
102	Barred Antshrike	137	Yellow-tufted Honeyeater
103	Ocellated Antthrush	138	Greater Racket-tailed Drongo
104	Peruvian Cock-of-the-Rock	139	Black-faced Woodswallow
105	Yellow-thighed Manakin	140	Satin Bower Bird
106	Scissor-tailed Flycatcher	141	Greater Bird of Paradise
107	Vermilion Flycatcher	142	Common Raven
108	Small-billed Elaenia	143	Magpie-Jay
109	White-tipped Plantcutter	144	Yellow-billed Oxpecker
110	Superb Lyrebird	144	Paradise Whydah
111	Crested Lark	146	House (English) Sparrow
112	Barn Swallow	147	Gouldian Finch
113	Scarlet Minivet	148	Evening Grosbeak
114	White-cheeked Bulbul	149	Yellow-throated Vireo
115	Red-backed Shrike	150	Akiapolaau
116	Bohemian Waxwing	151	Blackburnian Warbler
117	Gray Wagtail	152	Western Tanager
118	Cactus Wren	152	Paradise Tanager
119	Northern Mockingbird	154	Pyrrhuloxia
120	White-crested Laughingthrush	155	Painted Bunting
121	Silver-eared Mesia	156	Grasshopper Sparrow
122	Hermit Thrush	157	Spot-breasted Oriole
123	Blue Rock Thrush		
124	White-rumped Shama	158	Index

◀ Male Cock-of-the-Rock
Male Western Tanager▼

Introduction

Birds have interested men throughout human history. At first this interest was probably part of an awareness of nature based on human needs for food, clothing, and protection. As men gained free time to contemplate their surroundings—and birds are a conspicuous part of these surroundings—a deeper interest developed. People marveled at the flight of birds, enjoyed viewing their colors and hearing their calls, and were intrigued by the texture of their feathers. It was no accident that many of history's intellectual giants, such as Aristotle and Darwin, were curious about the birds around them and sought to learn something of them.

Time's passage has seen no abatement in the interest in birds, and these vertebrate animals are very popular in today's technological world. The popularity of birds curiously relates to man's "peculiarities" as a mammal. Unlike most mammals, which are drably colored, see poorly, depend greatly on their keen sense of smell, and are active at night, man has excellent color vision, garbing himself colorfully. His sense of smell is relatively poor, and he is active chiefly during the day. His senses thus are the same ones emphasized in birds, diurnal animals that see and hear very well, are often brightly colored, and have a weak sense of smell. Because we are "attuned" to birds, millions of people observe them, and many persons so engaged contribute to our knowledge of these animals.

Birds have been called feathered reptiles, or "glorified" reptiles, because they evolved from an ancient group of reptiles, and they show great structural similarities with these vertebrates. Such a characterization does justice to neither group, for reptiles and birds differ markedly in appearance, physiology, and habits. The forelimbs of birds are highly modified for flight, and their bodies bear feathers, unique structures even though derived from reptilian scales. Birds lay hard-shelled eggs that are incubated until hatching, have highly modified respiratory and circulatory systems, and are able to maintain a constant body temperature, a trait shared only with mammals. Their bones are thin and hollow. Feathers enable the flight of birds, act as insulation (thus penguins can swim in frigid Antarctic waters, and ravens can survive, with few mammals and no reptiles, in the high Arctic), and serve the functions of concealment and display. The "mouth" has evolved into a toothless, hard beak or bill; the bony, muscular tail is very reduced; other parts of the skeleton are fused or otherwise modified; and the lower legs and clawed toes are scale-covered, but reduced mainly to tendons, bones, and skin. The behavior of birds is often highly complex.

The outstanding development in the history of birds, which date back to the Jurassic Geological Period (more than 130 million years ago), was the evolution of their ability to fly. Flight opened to birds a great variety of habitats and ecological niches, previously unexploited or poorly exploited by other animals. Birds evolved, adapted, and gradually came to fill these various niches. They underwent extensive structural and physiological shifts, profoundly affecting their lives. As flying animals *par excellence,* birds have had their entire body and all its functions changed to accommodate flight. Wings evolved from the forelimbs of their reptilian ancestor, and feathers from the scales. The long wings are light because there is little flesh and muscle—bird "wings" that we see are the feather overcoat of a lightweight, bony frame. Through an intricate system of tendinous connections, the major flight muscles are situated on the body, near the center of gravity, and not on the wings where they would cause imbalance. The biting, chewing apparatus (teeth, heavy jaw muscles) of the bird's ancestor, and other associated structures of the head, have been lost or mod-

Earliest fossil bird, Archeopteryx

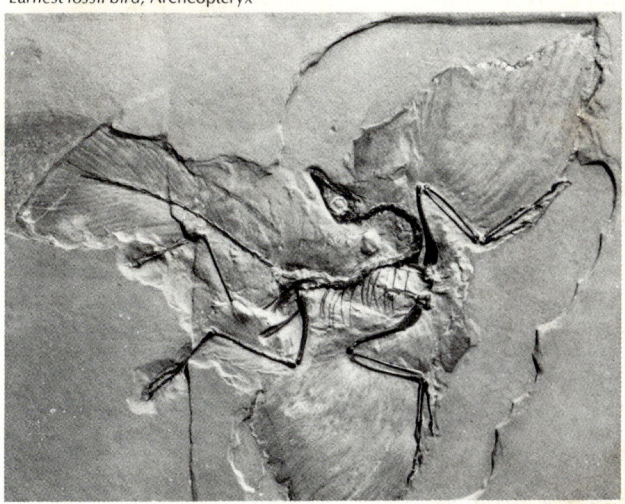

ified—the bird "chews" its food in its muscular stomach or gizzard. Again, weighty structures thus have been relocated from a position where they would interfere with flight to one nearer the center of gravity. The long, bony, muscular tail of other vertebrates is replaced by the feather "tail" that we see, the feathers being controlled by muscles at their bases, where the reduced, fused tailbone lies. Hollow, light bones of the body and limbs bear internal connections to the system of air sacs, which facilitate rapid breathing and insure the oxygen needed for the strenuous activity of flying. Birds' eyes are extremely well developed and capable of rapid adaptation, important in fast-flying animals that must accommodate rapidly, as when a bird passes from direct sunlight instantly into the dense, shady foliage of a tree. This list of structures and activities affected by flight can be extended further to include virtually every part of the bird's body and every activity.

Part of the fascination of birds is their often complex behavior, complex in terms of the stimuli to which they respond, the sense organs involved, the nervous system itself, and the appropriate and speedy muscular action that results. Examples of such behavior are the spectacular displays of birds of paradise and the building of decorated display structures by the bower birds; the intricate songs of thrushes, wrens, and lyrebirds; the extensive night migrations over the open ocean by wood-warblers; and the tightly woven nests of the weaverbirds. Most small birds are short-lived and have little time for learning, hence they tend to be fully prepared to carry out many functions at an

Crowned Pigeon

early age, nearly or entirely in their complete form. Most bird behavior patterns seem to have basic, non-modifiable components that are then embellished by the effects of experience. For example, bird song is often stereotyped in pattern, appearing at an appropriate time in life with no previous experience. There is, of course, a "built-in" limit of sounds that a particular species can produce. However, the pattern is frequently subject to modification at the time when the bird commences to sing. Local "dialects" may occur, all the singing males of an area producing phrases or elements found only in those populations, as well as individually specific elements that enable the birds to distinguish each other's songs. Birds of other species have critical learning periods, such as the time when they are still young birds in the nest, and the pattern of the male parent's song that they hear becomes fixed; when the young bird commences to breed, usually in the next year, this song may appear without practice or further experience. Alarm calls, location notes, and some other vocalizations are not usually subject to modification, but appear in full form under appropriate conditions in the life of young birds. Very complex behavior, such as the particular construction of a nest, the manner of binding together its materials, and specific migration habits, may be essentially unmodifiable. Humans, having highly modifiable behavior, may find it difficult to comprehend the stereotyped nature and often abrupt appearance of complicated patterns of bird behavior. It must be borne in mind, however, that many birds, especially smaller species, live to an age of only one to two years on the average. By very strict measures (i.e., through natural selection) nature

◀ Adult King Penguins
Male Ring-necked Pheasant ▼

has insured that birds "know" when and in what direction to migrate, for example, or how they must display to attract a mate. The penalty for failure is severe, and nature's weeding out of those that fail constantly sharpens the adaptation of species to their environment, for only successful birds survive, breed, and thus pass on the genetic attributes responsible for their success.

Within the rigid framework of life imposed upon them by their flight specializations, birds have adapted to diverse environments. They show remarkable variation in feeding habits and in the features of the bill, legs, and feet, structures directly involved in obtaining food. The hooked bill of an eagle, the spear-like bill of the heron, the delicate, long bill of the hummingbird, and the heavy, conical bill of the grosbeak are adapted for special food-gathering and food-rendering habits—meat eating, fish spearing, nectar sipping, and seed cracking. Legs and feet, too, broadcast the habits and habitats of birds. Large birds of marshes, swamps, and grasslands usually have long legs. Small birds that perch in grasses or trees have moderately short legs and small feet; the feet of birds are constructed so that the touch of a branch or twig causes the clasping of the toes and claws without conscious action, allowing a bird to sleep securely on a perch for the night, its feet locked around the branch. Hummingbirds, swifts, swallows, and other birds that spend most of the day in flight have very small feet and short legs. Eagles, hawks, and owls are strong-legged, the toes bearing large claws used in catching and killing their prey. Swimming birds such as pelicans and ducks have webs between the toes, and others such as grebes bear

Bill Adaptations
hummingbird
duck
flamingo
grosbeak
hawk
toucan

Feet Adaptations
coot
crane
gull
hawk

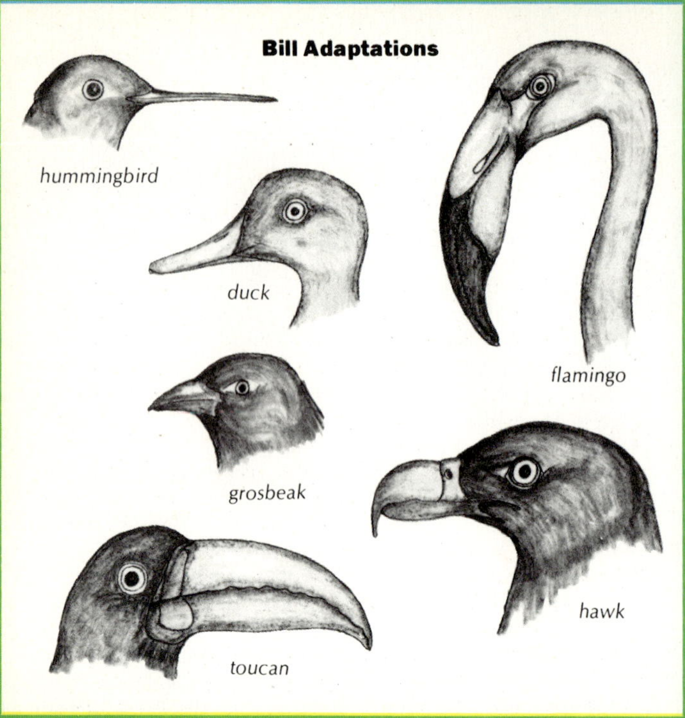

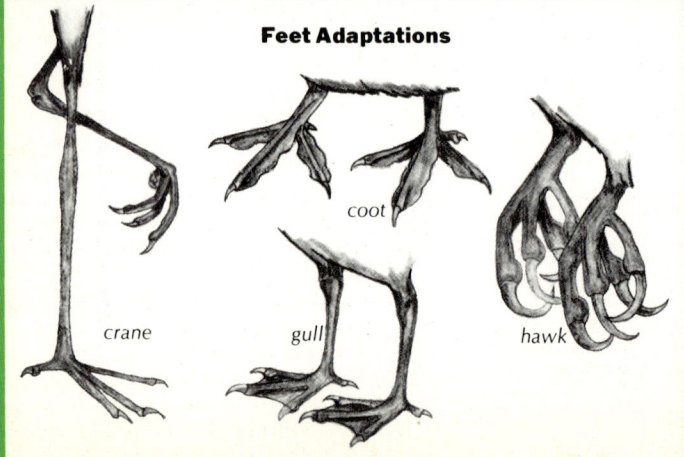

flattened lobes fringing the toes, features useful in propelling them through the water.

Their ability to fly has bestowed upon birds a remarkable mobility. They have been able to reach remote areas inaccessible to many other animals, crossing barriers such as seas and mountains, and exploiting favorable habitats where and as they developed through geological history. They also have been able to take advantage of their mobility in migrating to favorable, but only seasonally available, habitats, then flying elsewhere before conditions have become inhospitable. Migrant birds can utilize such areas as the Arctic tundras during the long days of summer when food is abundant, then fly southward to spend the rest of the year in other climes. The cold or dry climate or adverse weather conditions seem not to hamper birds very much in a direct way, but they do so indirectly by covering, killing, or otherwise affecting the food supply, for the energy needs of birds to sustain their activities are great, and they must have access to suitable foods or move elsewhere. Despite their great mobility, many birds, even some migratory species, tend to have restricted distributions, particularly in the breeding season. Such restrictions may be due to the presence of a closely related species in an adjacent, otherwise favorable area. (Related species are apt to have similar ecologies and be unable to coexist.) Or a species may be so specialized in its habits (diet, nesting requirements, etc.) that it is restricted to a relatively small area in which its needs are met. Only various seabirds, some species with restricted diets, and certain birds of very arid regions can be considered somewhat nomadic, wandering over great distances; but even these can be mainly classed as migratory, since they tend to return to certain areas in which they breed.

The sheer size of the world's human population, its ever-expanding needs, and man's awesome, often ecologically disastrous, uses of land and water are threatening many animals, even mobile birds. Survival of various birds often depends on specialized food and habitat requirements. Birds—all animals—tend to occupy fully all suitable environment that is accessible. Every habitat has a component biotic structure, including its complement of birds. When a habitat is modified, its bird fauna changes, but when a habitat is "developed" or destroyed, its birds effectively are killed. Perhaps unfortunately, we do not see them die, but this nevertheless happens. All surrounding, suitable areas have their

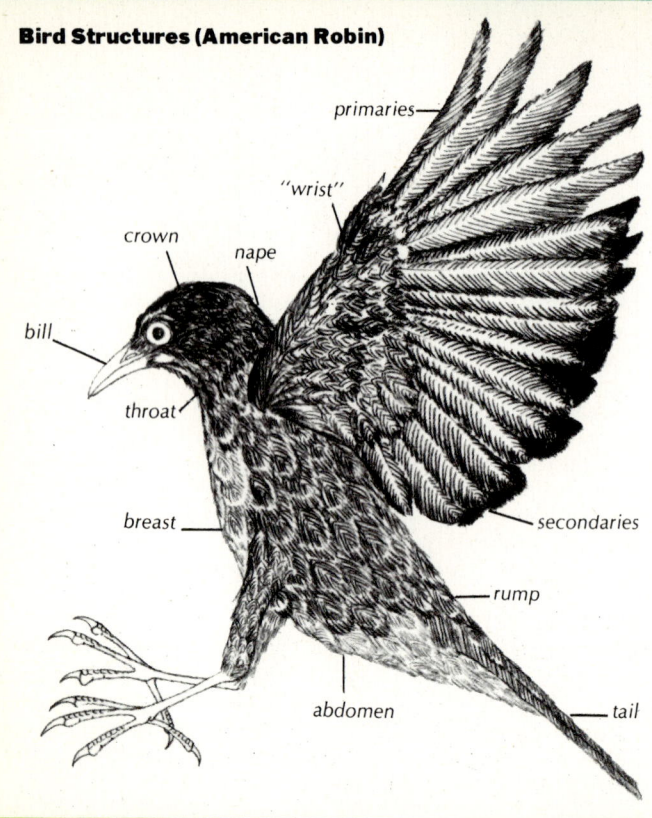

Bird Structures (American Robin)

own birds, usually better adapted to those areas than are any birds from outside. When an area is destroyed or highly modified, its evicted birds wander and ultimately perish; or, if they successfully displace other birds elsewhere, the net effect is the loss of the number of birds occupying the destroyed habitat. Loss of habitat is by far the single greatest threat to wildlife, including birds. Habitat loss is especially devastating on oceanic islands and in tropical forest regions, both of which are being changed wholesale and often without concerned, knowledgeable persons available to protest the destruction. But it is also severe in parts of developed countries that have already suffered great reduction of their natural environment. Sanctuaries are sometimes provided, and a

Skeleton of American Robin

lone wildlife sanctuary is better than no sanctuary; but if truly alone and of small size, it is little better than a zoo, and becomes an ever more expensive "zoo" to manage and protect. There must be sufficiently widespread, accessible habitats available to support viable bird populations. Restriction and fragmentation of habitats start the grim process of extinction, magnifying the problems of less numerous bird species by exposing them to ever-increasing and diverse hazards, hazards that may be as subtle as the disruption of nesting caused by the mere presence of people in the general area.

Of the hundreds of extinctions caused by direct and indirect actions of man in the past few hundred years, most have involved highly

Rufous-capped Antshrike with young at nest

specialized species. Collecting of its eggs and killing of the birds for food caused the extinction by 1844 of the Great Auk *(Pinguinus impennis)*, the largest of the auks and the only one that had lost its ability to fly. Millions of Passenger Pigeons *(Ectopistes migratorius)*, a very social species that nested in vast colonies, could still be found in North America a little more than a century ago, but market hunting in the nesting colonies reduced and scattered the birds, and by 1914 they were gone. Logging of highland pine forests and hunting of the birds by loggers and Indians, more out of curiosity (and for use of their bills as amulets) than for other reasons, may already have doomed the largest of all woodpeckers, the Imperial Ivorybill *(Campephilus imperialis)* of Mexico, and it is a moot point whether there still exist outside of Cuba (i.e., in the southeastern United States) individuals of the slightly smaller Ivory-billed Woodpecker *(Campephilus principalis)*. Man's introduction of cats, mongooses, goats, and other animals has eliminated from islands many species of birds not killed directly by man. Technological progress led to the use of fertilizers and pesticides that have rendered barren many seemingly favorable habitats and have systematically poisoned, thus reducing and threatening, many of the larger meat- and fish-eating birds (which of course tend to obtain easily available food, such as weakened, poisoned mice or fish).

Every swamp, forest, woodland, and lake that can be saved helps to perpetuate certain birds, and every step taken to reduce and eliminate hazardous pollutants also aids in preserving many species. In terms of the number of threatened species, the danger of extinction is greatest in developing tropical countries where the tendency is to squander forests for a mere pittance in short-term rewards, thus threatening their hundreds of forest birds, many of which are poorly known and apt to disappear before their plight is recognized. Preservation of the world's plants and animals is everyone's concern, for we are the custodians of these resources which are the heritage of not only present but future generations of men. Natural habitats should be saved not simply for preservation itself, but because they are natural reservoirs or banks from which posterity may draw and develop new domestic plants and animals, forest products, medicines, and other items: by destroying these banks we deprive future generations of new products and alternatives, and this deprivation could be fatal to humanity. It is my hope that this book will promote an awareness of birds and their needs, and that interested readers will be stimulated to act on behalf of bird preservation. It is important to note that, aside from their economic importance in controlling insects and other pests, and from the great interest they generate, they serve as a conspicuous reminder of our planet's health.

The classification of birds is currently in flux as far as the higher groups, or "taxa," are concerned. Structural similarities among birds are great, and differences (features upon which their classification is based) are rather small or involve structures that are readily acted upon by nature, hence posing confusing problems. The arrangement of families in this book generally follows the so-called Wetmore system (named after American ornithologist Alexander Wetmore), with some modification following recent research developments. There are fewer problems at lower classificatory levels, and these generally do not affect species treated here.

A species is an interbreeding or potentially interbreeding population unit, self-defined in that individuals of a species recognize each other as members of that species, selecting as mates only birds of their own species. There are about 9,000 species of birds in the world, many more than the number of mammals or reptiles. Each species has its unique Latinized name, always italicized, consisting of two parts, a generic (group) name that is capitalized and, following that, a species name that is never capitalized. The name identifies the species to anyone talking or writing of it, because international convention dictates that it is unique. Thus the name is universal, as compared with the common or vernacular name, which may vary, often even within one country or language. Closely related species form a genus. These genera are grouped into families, and the families into orders, which compose the chordate class Aves—birds. A species may of course have no living relative that is related sufficiently closely to be included in the same genus, and a very distinct species may form its own genus, or family, or rarely even a higher group by itself. For instance, the Secretarybird forms its own family, and the Ostrich has been placed in its own order.

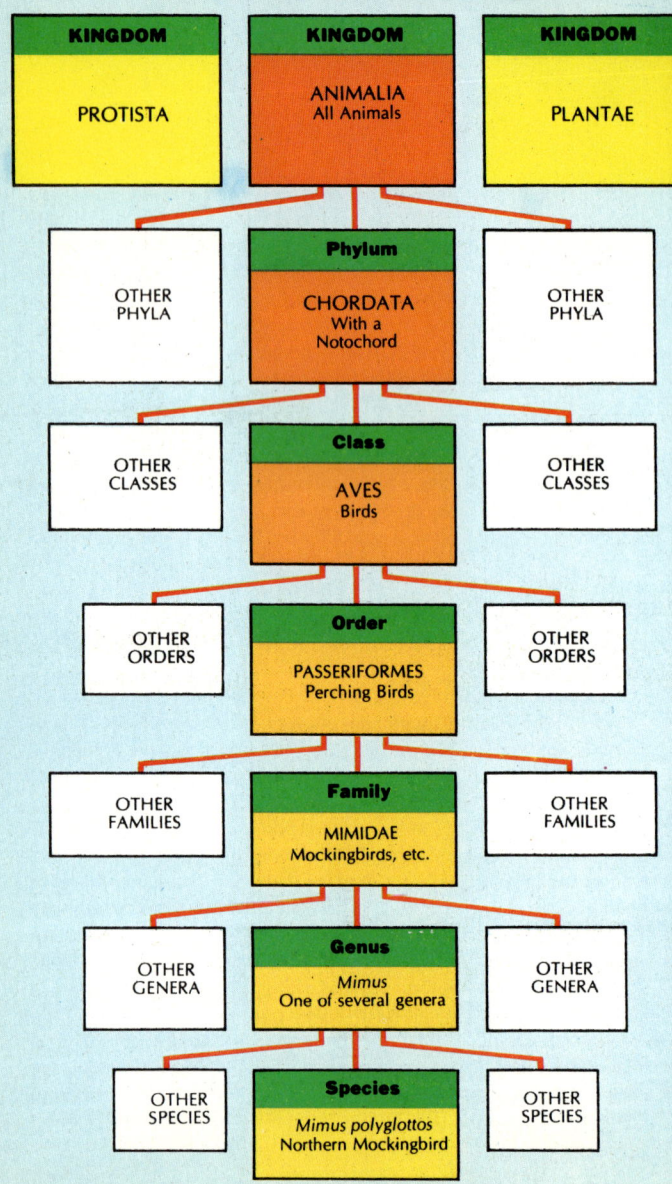

This book provides a brief vignette of species representing most of the major groups or families of birds. Each account contains a capsule life history of the species discussed, remarks concerning characteristics of its group, and unusual items of information about the species or the group. The name of the bird's family and its common and scientific names are given, with an indication of the size in inches (e.g., 20") of the bird, measured from the tip of the bill to the tip of the tail.

The selection of species to be included herein was based upon several factors. I sought a balance among familiar species, species representing diversity both among and within families, and birds of unusual habits. The availability of suitable photographs considerably narrowed the selection, for many birds have never been photographed in color, or their existing photographs are of poor quality or depict birds in odd poses, or unusual habitats (as behind bars in a zoo!). Limitations of space prevented inclusion of representatives of all bird families, the number and exact limits of which are at present the subject of considerable scientific discussion. I was forced to exclude some very small families in order to be able to include several species of some of the very large and diverse families. The 140 accounts treat 101 bird families, over two-thirds of the families of birds, and all large families are represented by at least one species. This coverage gives an overview of the structural, taxonomic, and ecological diversity of birds. Within a family selection often had to be made between familiar and unusual species. Many common birds are unusual in some respects, facilitating some choices. In instances posing a difficult choice, I generally chose the less familiar species on the basis that common, well-known species are dealt with in other readily available sources.

It has been my good fortune to observe personally many of the species discussed in the text during my ornithological investigations throughout the Americas, and in Africa, Australia, Asia, and Europe. Most areas in which I have studied have changed drastically within the past decade. Despite all efforts to interject reason in modifying and halting this onslaught, it seems inevitable that we will lose many birds in the next half-century. The interest, concern, and support needed to stem this tide and to acquire information about endangered and potentially endangered habitats and birds are urgent matters that merit the reader's thought and attention.

Crested Tinamou (14") family Tinamidae
Eudromia elegans

The 40 or so species of tinamous live on the ground in tropical forests, savannas, and scrublands of the Americas and in the temperate South American grasslands. They share certain skull features with flightless, ostrich-like birds, but have a keeled sternum (breastbone). Largely brownish in color like its relatives, the Crested Tinamou inhabits the dry brushlands of central and southern Argentina and adjacent Chile.

In the breeding season, the male, which is smaller than the female, maintains a large territory where he prepares a depression in soil beneath a bush for use as a nest. The females move about in small groups and mate successively with different males, laying eggs in their nests. The eggs, green with a glossy sheen characteristic of tinamous, number four to 12 per nest, up to six being contributed by any one female. The male incubates the eggs and cares for the young birds with little or no help from females.

Leaves, seeds, flowers, and some insects form the diet of this tinamou. Apparently no water is taken directly, but is obtained from plant foods, and perhaps, in the young, from ingestion of fecal material of adults. Tinamous are hunted for food, their meat being widely acclaimed.

Ostrich *(72") family Struthionidae*
Struthio camelus

The open savannas, plains, and scrublands of Africa are the home of the largest living bird, the flightless Ostrich. Distinguished from South American rheas and Australian emus by its two (rather than three) toes, the Ostrich progresses effortlessly, and if necessary rapidly, through the grasslands on its strong legs and feet. Up to 8 feet tall, males are black and white, and use the wing and tail plumes in display; the smaller females are gray-brown and white.

Social except when nesting, they travel in small bands, picking up plant and animal items of food from the ground. Males at times employ a lion-like roar. The nest is a scratched depression in the soil, in which eight to 12 or more eggs are laid. Both sexes incubate the large eggs, the more conspicuous male mainly doing so at night.

Once ranging to Arabia, Ostriches are becoming ever more restricted to the large African parks that hopefully will sustain them so that they can continue to be observed in the wild.

Common Rhea (45") family Rheidae
Rhea americana

This family of large, flightless birds is represented by two South American species: the Common Rhea of the pampas and savannas of Argentina, Uruguay, and Brazil, and the Darwin's Rhea *(Pterocnemia pennata)*. Rheas have three toes, a small head, and feathering on the neck, unlike the considerably larger African Ostrich. Various plants and small animals make up their diet.

Male Common Rheas are larger than females and call loudly to attract prospective mates. A male may gather up to a half-dozen hens, which accompany him about and lay their cream-colored eggs in a nest he has scraped in the soil and lined with grasses. Up to three dozen eggs of his several mates are laid in the nest, and then the male drives away the females and undertakes the incubation of the eggs. They hatch in about six weeks, whereupon the young are escorted about, brooded, and protected by the male until they become independent.

About 5 feet tall, rheas are fast and can outrun a horse on a straight course; but their fleetness does not protect them from hunting, the collecting of their eggs for food, and the continued and increasing cultivation of their grassland habitat by man. Hence their numbers are diminishing.

Emu (72") family Dromiceidae
Dromiceus novaehollandiae

The Australian region's contribution to the world's array of large, flightless birds is composed of the Emu, and three related species of cassowaries (family Casuariidae). Between the Ostrich and Common Rhea in size, Emus are up to 6 feet tall, have three toes, quite massive legs, a partly feathered neck, and dense feathering caused by feather "aftershafts," which in effect make each feather a double feather. They move about the deserts, grasslands, and savannas of Australia in small groups and are able to run at great speed if danger threatens.

The larger males pair with females, which are smaller but similar in color, and ground nests of grass and leaves are arranged to hold as many as ten deep-green, rough-textured eggs. The male incubates the eggs, but after hatching both parents escort and protect the attractively striped young. Fruits, seeds, and insects form the diet of the Emu, which is diminishing in numbers but is less threatened than the Ostrich or Common Rhea.

▲ *At nest with eggs*

Kiwi or Brown Kiwi (26") family Apterygidae
Apteryx australis

New Zealand and adjacent islands are the home of the three kiwis, among the strangest of birds. Weighing up to seven pounds and standing barely a foot high, these short-necked, long-billed birds have hair-like feathering, long bristles about the face, no tail, mere stubs of wings, and short, powerful legs with four toes on each foot. They are unable to fly, and are active only at night. Skulking about the wet ground in damp, dense forests, they use the bill to probe into the soil and rotten logs; their nostrils are near the tip of the bill, and apparently kiwis employ a keen sense of smell in detecting worms, grubs, and berries that form their diet.

The Kiwi is the largest and most widespread species. Males are smaller than females and give a shrill call responsible for the native (Maori) name "kiwi"; females utter a hoarser call. The one or occasionally two eggs, enormous for the size of the bird, are laid in a natural burrow or one dug by the birds. The male builds the nest and incubates the egg(s) without help from his mate. The egg hatches in about 75 days, and after several days in which it gradually gains strength, the hatchling moves out to begin probing for worms on its own.

Red-throated Loon or Diver *(25")* family Gaviidae
Gavia stellata

Diving birds *par excellence* are the four species of loons or divers, all northern, tundra-nesting species. Clumsy on land with their legs so far to the rear, these spear-billed, webbed-footed birds swim masterfully, and are usually found in or beside the water. The sexes are alike in color, and there is a drastic shift from colorful breeding to drab winter plumage. The Red-throated Loon or Diver has an uptilted bill, and in the breeding season its head is gray, its neck striped, and its throat rusty.

This loon builds a nest of vegetation near or in the water, or simply lays its eggs in a depression in the ground. Two deep olive-brown eggs are laid, and the hatchlings quickly make for the nearest water. Both parents tend the young, which may ride about on their backs.

Red-throated Loons feed on fishes and various invertebrates. They winter along continental seacoasts as far south as the fringe of the subtropics.

On nest

Great Crested Grebe *(18") family Podicipedidae*
Podiceps cristatus

The Great Crested Grebe is one of the large members of this highly aquatic, cosmopolitan, but small—18 species—bird family. Grebes have their legs set far back on the body, giving them difficulty when walking on land; their wings are short, the tail almost lacking, the blade-like legs are compressed laterally, and the toes are webbed in lobes about the segments of each toe, with connections to adjacent toes at the base. They tend to be brownish above and pale below, and often have distinct breeding and non-breeding plumages, although the sexes are similar in color.

Aptly called "helldivers" in some areas, they can submerge gradually from a buoyant, floating position, until perhaps only the head is out of the water; or they can dive rapidly, to reappear farther away or, more likely, to come up in reeds out of sight of an intruder.

The Great Crested Grebe has a spectacular mutual display during courtship, in which the male and female speed toward each other with necks outstretched, then pull upright inches apart, crests erect, and often dangling algae or weeds from the bill as part of the display.

Emperor Penguin *(48") family Spheniscidae*
Aptenodytes forsteri

Penguins fascinate young and old with their antics, their short, dense feathers that give a fur-like appearance, their upright posture on land, and their black-and-white, "formal" coloration. Natural swimmers, they essentially fly underwater using their wings, which have flattened, modified bones and bear no flight feathers, as flippers, although they are unable to fly in the air.

The Emperor is the largest of the penguins, standing nearly 4 feet high. Entirely dependent upon fishes and squid and other oceanic invertebrates for food, the Emperor Penguins leave the water for pairing, often many miles inland on the Antarctic ice. After mating, which they do in the southern fall, the single egg is laid, then placed by the male on his feet. While the female goes off to the ocean to feed, the male huddles, the egg always held on his feet snugly against his body and surrounded by feathers, and he thus incubates the egg for the two months or so required to hatch it. His fat reserves sustain him in the dark and cold of the winter until the egg hatches. The female then returns, fat and bearing large quantities of food, and the male goes to the sea for several weeks of recuperation and food gathering. The adults alternate at bringing food for the nearly four months of growth near the hatching site, before adults and young leave for the ocean, which they reach in the spring when food is abundant.

Other penguins occur on Antarctica, and along coasts and on islands as far as the Galapagos Islands off Ecuador to the north, near the Equator, but in a cold-water current.

Sliding on ice ▲
◀ *Brooding young*

25

Laysan Albatross (32") family Diomedeidae
Diomedea immutabilis

Albatrosses are large seabirds with fully webbed feet, long wings, and a complex bill, hooked at the tip and with the nostrils at the tips of "tubes" along the side of the bill. The largest species, the Wandering Albatross *(Diomedea exulans),* has a wingspread of 11 feet, the greatest of any living bird. Their wings beat rarely as they sail over the waves in windier areas of the southern oceans. Of the 14 species, only three enter the northern oceans. One of these, the Laysan, lives in the North Pacific, nesting at a few islands, notably at Midway Island, where a long-term confrontation between the albatrosses, represented by conservationists, and the U.S. Navy has resulted in compromise measures that have preserved the nesting colonies.

The five- to six-pound, dark-backed Laysan Albatross does not begin its breeding until it is five to ten years of age. Feeding mainly on squids, it sails the North Pacific vastness, but "young" birds three years old and older may drop in on the breeding colony and begin forming pairs one or two years before they actually nest. Breeding begins in November, eggs hatch in January and February, and the young are tended by one or another parent until June or July or even August. The egg is incubated in a feather-formed pouch, against the bare skin. After the single egg is laid in sand, the nest is built by the incubating bird which reaches out to pull in vegetation and sand within reach, scraping up a rim that may be 10 inches high.

Sooty Shearwater *(17") family Procellariidae*
Puffinus griseus

About 55 species of shearwaters ply the oceans—mostly of the Southern Hemisphere—for much of the year. They have "tube-noses," that is, their nostrils open onto the bill from tubes on top of the bill. The Sooty is one of the larger species and, as the name indicates, is blackish in color, pale to white below, and with white "linings" that show under the wings in flight; the narrow hooked bill is dark, as are the legs. They glide low over the waves, frequently landing in the sea, then diving to catch fish, crustaceans, squids, and cuttlefish that make up their diet.

Sooty Shearwaters migrate to the Northern Hemisphere during the southern winter, returning to their nesting colonies in the islands near the tip of South America, along the Chilean coast, and near New Zealand and Australia. Pairs excavate a burrow up to 3 yards long, often at the base of a rock or shrub, and sometimes several miles from the sea. The single egg is laid usually on a lining of grasses, leaves, and sticks, and is incubated by both parents. After hatching early in the year, the young are fed during the night by the parents. Eerie loud sounds made by the great numbers of adults passing to and from the nesting colonies frightened sailors in the past. The young leave the colony after about 100 days of development and migrate northward, not to return to breed until they are three years old.

Wilson's Petrel *(7") family Hydrobatidae*
Oceanites oceanicus

This common petrel of the southern oceans migrates to the North Atlantic and may be seen from ships during much of the year. The "storm petrels" of this family are small in size and have webbed feet and a hooked bill with nostrils enclosed in tubes atop the bill, both nostrils combining into one opening. Wilson's Petrels are sooty black in color, somewhat smaller than a Robin *(Turdus migratorius)*; they have long black legs and toes, with golden webs between the toes, and a broad white area around the tail both above and below. They feed on crustaceans, small fishes, and refuse of all types tossed overboard from ships, which they follow for long distances. Dainty, they flutter just above the water, dangling their feet possibly to maintain the body in a position favorable for feeding.

Nesting takes place on islands of the South Atlantic and Indian oceans, south to the Antarctic Circle. A single egg is laid under a rock or in a crevice, in a nest lined with plant materials or feathers. Both adults take turns at incubating for 35 days or so. After hatching, the young bird remains at the nest site, fed by the adults, until April, when it leaves the island. The young of the year tend to migrate northward near the coast (South America), while the adults range far out in the ocean.

Red-tailed Tropicbird (30") family Phaethontidae
Phaethon rubricaudus

Three species of tropicbirds, or bosunbirds (boatswainbirds) as they are known familiarly to sailors, form another family of pelican-like birds. These web-footed birds have a dagger-shaped bill and elongated middle tail feathers. The Red-tailed Tropicbird is white, often with a pinkish cast, black about the face and in the wings, and it has a red bill and long, red, streamer-like middle tail feathers that twist and bend as the bird flies. Graceful, accomplished flyers, often found far at sea, these tropicbirds dive from a height of 20 to 40 feet into the ocean to capture squids or fishes.

Nesting takes place on various islands about Australia, and in the South Pacific and Indian oceans. A single egg is laid in a scrape under a ledge, in cliff crevices, or under a bush. The young hatches bearing a coat of down feathers, unlike the young of related pelicans and cormorants. Both parents incubate the egg and tend the chick, feeding it first a diet of squids and other cephalopods and later adding bony fishes. Nesting colonies are often active throughout the year, new pairs moving in as others complete their breeding.

◀ *At nest*

Red-footed Booby (30") family Sulidae
Sula sula

Related to the pelicans and cormorants are the ten species of boobies or gannets, strong-flying, heavy-bodied seabirds with large, fully webbed feet. The bill, which is strong and pointed, is employed in seizing fish and squid obtained by the pursuing booby after a dive of 50, 70, or even 100 feet into the water. Boobies are very social, nesting in great colonies and moving about in flocks.

The Red-footed Booby is a small species, mainly white in color, although there are gray and brown phases. This booby is peculiar in its family in that it seems to be active at night (its eyes are correspondingly larger than those of other boobies), and its nesting requirements include a need for trees or bushes—hence many barren or rocky tropical islands used by related species are shunned by the Red-foot.

The one or two young hatch naked in their tree nest and must be protected from exposure to the hot sun until their downy feathers grow in. The chief food of this booby consists of flyingfishes; these are swallowed, then later regurgitated by the nesting adults to feed the young.

Great Cormorant *(35") family Phalacrocoracidae*
Phalacrocorax carbo

The 30 species of cormorants inhabit the seacoasts, rivers, and lakes of most parts of the world. Fish-eaters like their kin the pelicans and Anhingas, the cormorants have a rather narrow bill with a hook at the tip. They swim in the water, and dive to pursue their finny quarry. After obtaining a fish, they turn it about in the bill so that it can be swallowed headfirst (to prevent catching the sharp fins in the throat), and then they often fly to a perch where they spread their wings, drying them.

The Great Cormorant is a large species and the most widespread of its family, occurring from Nova Scotia to Europe, Africa, Asia, and Australia. Nesting in large colonies on cliffs or in trees, Great Cormorants cough up or regurgitate fishes they have swallowed to feed their young, who jab their bills deep into the parent's maw to extract a choice bit of food. Adults and young readily disgorge foul-smelling, partly digested food when they are disturbed, discouraging intruders into the nesting colony. Nesting and roosting areas of several species of cormorants that congregate in vast numbers provide large quantities of "guano," their excreta, harvested commercially for fertilizer.

The Great Cormorant was used for centuries by Chinese and Japanese fishermen in catching fish; working on a "leash" with a loop about the bird's throat to prevent its swallowing the catch, the cormorants seized fish that the fishermen then took from them.

In nesting colony, Kenya

"Drying" wings after swimming

Anhinga *(35") family Anhingidae*
Anhinga anhinga

A denizen of wooded swamps and fresh-water ponds and lakes in the tropics and adjacent areas of the New World, the Anhinga has close relatives, possibly of the same species, in Africa and Asia. Called "darters" in the Old World and often known as "snakebirds" in the Americas, Anhingas are large, cormorant-like birds with a long, thin neck and a pointed bill. These birds forage for fishes and other vertebrate and invertebrate animals in the water, spearing them with the sharp bill, then shaking and banging them against a branch.

Their feathers are not fully "waterproof," and they often spread their wings for a while after swimming. While in the water they sometimes swim with only the curved neck and head projecting from the water. Their feet are fully webbed between the toes.

Nesting pairs seek the company of other Anhingas and various herons and build a nest consisting of a large platform of sticks, usually over water. The three or four chalky-blue eggs are incubated by both sexes, and both adults feed the young by regurgitation. Males are glossy greenish-black with grayish-white markings in the wings; females are brownish. Anhingas are often seen to fly about, gliding and circling, apparently aimlessly.

White Pelican *(65") family Pelecanidae*
Pelecanus onocrotalus

All but one of the world's six pelicans are mainly white in color, and these include the eastern European, African, and Asian White Pelican. Large birds with fully webbed feet (webs connect all four toes), pelicans are well known for their long, hook-tipped bill that bears a large, drooping pouch, used to catch and to hold numbers of fish. These are caught by the bird either swimming and scooping or by diving from a height of 30 or 40 feet. At times a group of pelicans work together in attacking schools of fish at the surface, encircling them or driving them into shallow water.

Nesting White Pelicans show a tinge of pink in their plumage. They breed in fresh-water marshes, constructing a bulky nest in reedbeds, numbers of birds nesting colonially. Up to four eggs are laid and incubated for 30 days or so. The young are fed regurgitated fish from the adults' bills, and soon they are thrusting their bill deep into the maw of the adult bill to drag out fishes.

Pelicans have suffered serious declines in numbers throughout the world due to toxic effects of some pollutants. It is hoped that these distinctive, comical, and interesting birds can be preserved.

Magnificent Frigatebird (38") family Fregatidae
Fregata magnifica

The five frigatebirds, or man-o'-war birds as they sometimes are called, ply the tropical seacoasts and many oceanic islands of the world. They have a forked tail, a hooked beak, and very long wings that sustain them in their marvelous flight antics. Frigatebirds rarely if ever alight on the water, but wheel above the sea searching for fish, squid, or other sea life. They also look for fishing birds such as boobies or pelicans that they can harass and badger into regurgitating and dropping food they have swallowed—the frigatebirds swooping gracefully to recover the disgorged food before it hits the water.

The Magnificent Frigatebird, largest of the family, is long-lived, taking five years to reach maturity. Found in the Central and South Atlantic, and along the Pacific Coast of the Americas, this species nests in colonies near those of other seabirds. The all-black male proclaims his territory atop a bush, inflating a bright-red throat pouch, or circles over the bush with the pouch inflated. The larger, white-bellied female gathers sticks for the nest while the male remains at the site to protect it, for other frigatebirds are quick to steal the twigs if the nest is unattended. A single white egg is laid, and both adults incubate it and attend the young hatchling.

Black Swan (50") family Anatidae
Cygnus atratus

The waterfowl include nearly 150 species of ducks, geese, and swans in the family Anatidae, and three peculiar goose-like birds, the screamers, in the family Anhimidae. Ducks generally have a flattened bill with serrations along the edges, fairly short legs, and webbed feet. The screamers differ in a number of ways: in their molt; in their feet being webbed only at the base of the toes; in having air passages in most of the bones; and in having bony spurs on the wings.

The long-necked, large swans generally are white, but the Black Swan of Australia is an exception. Gray-black over most of its body, it has white markings in the wings, red eyes, and a white-banded red bill. Females resemble males but have somewhat shorter necks. Pairs are strongly territorial, but under favorable conditions, their territories may be small so that they may appear to be colonial. Four to ten eggs are laid in a large nest constructed in the rainy season; because the rains are irregular, Black Swans are prone to nest when there is rain, and thus nesting takes place at varying times in different areas. Unlike most waterfowl, the male assists the female during the five weeks of incubation. The young are well cared for by the aggressive, protective parents.

Black Swans frequent fresh-water ponds and lakes and salt-water lagoons, feeding on invertebrate animals and plant materials. They make a humming noise with the wings in flight; their trumpeting and bugling calls, used in courtship and territorial defense, are frequently heard at night.

At nest

Female Male

Mallard (23") family Anatidae
Anas platyrhynchos

One of the most abundant and widely distributed of the ducks, the Mallard represents the "puddle" or "dabbling" ducks that one sees tipping their tails up and dunking their heads under water in a quest for food. The wild ancestor of most strains of domestic ducks, the Mallard ranges around the Northern Hemisphere and seems at home equally in a large lake or estuary, and in a tiny prairie pothole.

Pairing occurs through an intricate series of displays and reactions on the wintering grounds. Once the northward migrating pairs reach the breeding grounds, however, the female goes off by herself to find a concealed place in which she builds a nest of grass and weeds and lays her five to 12 greenish eggs. These are covered with down from her body and are carefully incubated and tended until hatching. The downy young move to the water, to be led about and protected by the mother until they are independent.

Mallards feed on diverse plant materials, including seeds (especially of grasses and grains), roots and stems of various plants, nuts, fruits, earthworms, insects, crayfish, and other items, including bread tossed to them at countless ponds in northern countries. Where fed regularly, they habituate readily to man, their antics providing great pleasure as well as affording the careful observer with instructive situations for the study of behavior.

Smew (17") family Anatidae
Mergus albellus

The Smew is a woodland swamp, bog, and lake duck of Europe and Siberia, the Old World counterpart of the North American Hooded Merganser *(Mergus cucullatus)*. Mergansers are fish- and insect-eating ducks, narrow of body, with thin, saw-like edges of the bill that are useful in seizing and holding fish. The largely white and black male Smew has greenish-black marks on the face, crest, and sides of the breast, a white wing patch, and gray on the sides and tail; the more somber female is mostly gray with a brown head and white cheeks.

In courtship, males give grunting and whistling sounds with an intricate array of actions, including a head-flinging display in which the body ends up mostly out of the water. The female quacks and responds actively to the male. The six to nine eggs are laid in a cavity within a tree or in a nest box, where they are incubated for 30 days. The young ducklings flutter down from the nest to nearby water in about ten weeks. Approximately at this time the adult males undergo molt into the very female-like, so-called "eclipse" plumage, which they wear for a very short time before molting into their typical attire.

Smews eat mainly water insects and their larvae, but they take some fishes. They migrate southward for the winter, reaching the Mediterranean region and Japan but generally avoiding salt water.

Greater Flamingo (46") family Phoenicopteridae
Phoenicopterus ruber

The four species of flamingos are distributed about the warm areas of the Americas, southern Eurasia, Africa, and southwestern Asia. Large birds, flamingos have long, thin legs and a long neck, webbed toes, and a distinctive bill that is abruptly bent downward in the middle and has duck-like flanges along its sides. The bill functions as a strainer: it is held upside down in water or mud and the thick tongue works within the opening and closing, comb-edged bill, pumping to strain out small invertebrate animals and plants, which are then swallowed.

The Greater Flamingo is the most widespread species, and the largest. Depending on location, it varies in color from white to light red, but always shows at least some pink. Yellow-eyed, with a black-tipped bill and black-tipped wings, the Greater Flamingo is highly social throughout the year, and the huge flocks of these rosy-hued birds, flying with legs and neck extended, are an impressive sight in the lake areas or coastal lagoons where they congregate.

Courting displays involve "saluting" with the brilliant wings and much rushing about, usually by large groups of flamingos. Pairs nest in large colonies, the females scooping up mud and erecting a mud "hill," up to 20 inches or more in height, scooped out in the center. When this nest dries out, the one or, rarely, two white eggs are laid in it.

Standing on back of water buffalo ▶

Cattle Egret *(17") family Ardeidae*
Bubulcus ibis

A straight, pointed bill, special neck modifications that permit a double, S-like curvature, a comb-like middle toe claw, and the presence of several pairs of powder down patches characterize the 60 or so species of herons. (Powder downs are modified feathers that grow continuously and fragment at the tips into powdery material that the bird uses to condition normal feathers.)

The Cattle Egret is a medium-sized heron originally found in southern Eurasia, Africa, and Indonesia, but which has managed to colonize and spread throughout the Americas and more recently, Australia, mainly without the aid of man. Adapted to feeding among large mammals, it was predisposed to benefit from man's agriculture, particularly cattle raising. Groups of these white birds follow closely or even precede a moving cow, seizing insects that are forced into flight. They may perch on the backs of mammals, perhaps eating ticks found there. They are not entirely dependent on such animals, however, for they seek food on their own in dry pastures and in ponds, eating, in addition to grasshoppers, crickets, and other insects, frogs and fishes.

Nesting within rookeries including other herons, the male Cattle Egrets steal sticks from related species and carry them to the females, who build the nest, which requires some 200 sticks for its construction. Two to six eggs are laid and incubated by both parents for the 25 or so days until hatching.

Shoebill or Whale-headed Stork (46") family Balaenicipitidae
Balaeniceps rex

The only member of its family, the Shoebill is generally considered distantly related to the storks (Ciconiidae). Like herons, however, it has patches of powder down (like that of the Cattle Egret) and flies with its neck folded rather than stretched out as do storks. Its bill is very deep and wide, with a nail-like hook at the tip. The Shoebill inhabits the extensive marshes in the upper White Nile River region of east-central Africa, where it stalks about or stands quietly, feeding on fishes, frogs, and reptiles. Like the storks, Shoebills rattle their bills in certain displays. A reed or grass nest is built in a dry part of the marsh, and two eggs form the clutch.

As peculiar in appearance and also puzzling as to its relationships but much more widely distributed in the African region, the smaller, brown Hammerhead *(Scops umbretta)* is also placed in a family of its own. The Hammerhead has a long crest and a flattened but long bill. It combines some features of the herons and of storks, but is distinctive—it nests in a huge compartmented structure of sticks plastered with mud, built in a tree or on a rock face. The small entry hole is hidden beneath or at one side of the nest and is slick with mud, affording an entrance only for the adept owners.

Scarlet Ibis *(22") family Threskiornithidae*
Eudocimus ruber

About 30 species comprise this family of ibises and spoonbills, relatives of the herons that have the long bill curved downward or flattened rather than pointed and straight. They also lack the powder downs (see Cattle Egret) and fly with the neck outstretched rather than folded back. The Scarlet Ibis of northern and eastern South America is one of the most beautiful of the family with its scarlet plumage and bare red face and legs. Only its black wingtips and dark eyes and bill break the red pattern of coloration. Young birds, which are brown and white, do not acquire the adult red plumage until three years of age. Various foods—crustaceans, worms, mollusks, insects, and fishes—are obtained from the lagoons and pools and surrounding muddy areas. These birds wander widely in the dry season, even feeding on dry grasslands.

Nesting occurs in the wet season, in large, widely scattered colonies on mangrove islands along the coast or in dense flooded forest patches of inland savannas. Because of the inaccessibility of such areas, the species is little known, unlike its very similar relative the White Ibis *(Eudocimus albus)*, with which it associates. Two or three blotched eggs are placed in a stick nest constructed in dense trees over water. The young inserts its long bill into that of the adult to feed. Unusual in the family are the spoonbills, including the pink-and-white Roseate Spoonbill *(Platalea ajaja)*, which ranges from South America to the southern United States. Its flattened, spoon-tipped bill is used for feeding in sweeping, side-to-side swings through the water.

Saddlebill Stork *(56") family Ciconiidae*
Ephippiorhynchus senegalensis

The stately, colorful Saddlebill is larger than the White Stork *(Ciconia ciconia)* of Europe, the baby-bringing stork of myth. White-bodied with black wings, legs, and neck and head, it has red "knees" (actually ankles) and a red bill, black in the middle and bearing a yellowish, casque-like "saddle" on top at the base. Males have brown eyes and females yellow.

Found in the more open areas of Africa, the Saddlebill forages in marshy grasslands, usually in pairs. Once mated, the adults stay paired and there is little courtship behavior. One display involves the frantic dashing of one bird to and fro through the water before its mate; the displaying bird then runs to its mate and stops with its wings spread widely. The nest is constructed in a tree, and three eggs are laid.

Sharing the African range of the Saddlebill is the Marabou or Adjutant Stork *(Leptoptilos crumeniferus)*, a huge-billed bird with a pinkish neck wattle that vies with vultures and hyaenas at the kills of lions and subsists often by scavenging. Fourteen other storks occur around the world, largely favoring tropical areas.

Andean Condor *(42") family Cathartidae*
Vultur gryphus

This family of vultures is restricted to the Americas, although fossils from Europe indicate a formerly more extensive distribution. Some features of these scavengers are a naked head; nostrils that are connected within the bill; feathers lacking an aftershaft (secondary shaft); and lack of a syrinx (the structure largely responsible for bird vocalizations). The Andean Condor is the largest vulture, weighing up to 25 pounds and having a wingspread of up to 10½ feet. Fortunately, it is more common than its relative, the endangered California Condor, *(Vultur californianus)*, which numbers 60 or fewer individuals restricted to a small area of California.

The Andean Condor enhances the majesty of the Andes Mountains from Venezuela and Colombia to the southern tip of South America. In Peru these condors fly to the coast and beyond to island seabird colonies, where they break the eggs and suck the contents of such eggs that they find. Generally condors feed on carrion, dead or perhaps dying animals; there is argument over whether they prey upon newly born mammals.

Nesting in loose colonies, the condors place their single egg on a cliff ledge in the mountains. If the young hatches and develops to adulthood, the adults nest only every two years, since it takes over a year of care before young birds are independent. In some parts of the Andes, as in Bolivia, one can still see up to 30 or more of these magnificent birds soaring together, almost effortlessly, on the updrafts.

Osprey *(23") family Pandionidae*
Pandion haliaetus

Distributed widely about the world, the Osprey is the sole member of its family. It looks like a hawk (Accipitridae) but has distinctive anatomical features and resembles the New World vultures (Cathartidae) in feather arrangement. It has a reversible outer toe and pointed scales beneath its toes, both traits of use in fishing. Virtually all of its diet is fish of sizes up to four pounds. An Osprey may perch on a branch over water or actively fly about above the water seeking fish; spying one, it will hover, then dive with wings closed, grasping the fish in its long talons. Ospreys frequent rivers, lakes, and seacoasts all over the Northern Hemisphere, south to Mexico, southern Africa, and Australia, and migrate to coasts throughout the Southern Hemisphere.

In spring courtship, accompanied by several displays, takes place. Both sexes construct the nest, which is used year after year and which may be built in a tree, on a crag, or on the ground, the female doing most of the building while the male gets sticks. Three eggs are usually laid, incubated mainly or entirely by the female, which is fed by her mate. After about 35 days the eggs hatch; the female remains at the site for a month, and the male supplies the food. The young mature at three years. Possibly because of poisons in pesticide residues, the Osprey has become rare in certain areas.

Lammergeyer or Bearded Vulture (44") family Accipitridae
Gypaetus barbatus

This large family contains the 200-odd hawks, eagles, kites, and vultures (except New World vultures, Cathartidae) found throughout the world. The Lammergeyer is a large, tawny-breasted, bristly faced, brown-backed, vulture-like bird of the mountains of Africa and from southern Europe east to Tibet. Lammergeyers soar about their mountain crags, seeking carrion of all types. They may at times take live animals and have been noted digging insects from dung heaps. Their specialty is bones, which they may swallow whole; larger bones may be carried to favored rocky sites where they are split open. The Lammergeyer has a blunt, angled tongue that enables it to scoop out the marrow.

Pairs form in late fall in Europe, and nesting occurs during late winter. The courtship performance includes an eagle-like twisting, diving, swerving flight in front of the nest site, punctuated by screams as the birds may turn over completely. The one to two eggs are laid in a cave or ledge nest made of sticks, lined with wool, hair, and dung, and measuring up to 8 feet across. Both parents brood the young and incubate the eggs, although this task may fall to the female alone in some regions. The incubation period is about 53 days, and the young seem to remain about the nest even beyond the five to six months it takes for them to fledge and become self-sufficient.

Northern Goshawk (22") family Accipitridae
Accipiter gentilis

This large Northern Hemisphere representative of the 50 or so species of *Accipiter* was widely used in falconry during the Middle Ages. Its short, round wings and long tail assist it in its dashing, swerving flights through trees and brush after prey, which include squirrels, rabbits, young hares, mice, and birds up to the size of large grouse. Relentless and fierce in its chase, it may pursue its quarry to the feet of a surprised human onlooker.

The sexes are nearly alike in coloring, brownish-gray above, in a broad stripe through the eye, and in bars on white below, but females are as much as 65 percent larger than males: this usually is the case in birds of prey, but the difference in size is rarely so pronounced. Both sexes cackle, the female more deeply.

In spring the female returns to the nest of the previous year and screams to attract its mate. Both soar together or alone over the nest, the male diving and swooping, and they repair the nest or the male builds a new one. The nest, which is high in a tree and composed of sticks, is attended by the female, which is fed by the male. Usually three eggs are laid in April, May, or, in the far north, June. The female incubates them for the 37 or so days until hatching. The female does little hunting, but remains near or at the nest while the male hunts; she feeds the young, but only after the male leaves—a special scream serves to hasten him on his way. The young fly at 45 days and are independent at about 70 days.

Goshawks migrate, often irruptively when their food supply fails, as it does in the north in certain years.

Secretarybird *(55") family Sagittariidae*
Sagittarius serpentarius

In African grasslands and open areas one may see, striding about and often stopping to stamp its feet a bit, a 4-foot tall, long-legged bird with a gray body and tail, black wings, thighs and crest, and an orangish area about the eyes. The Secretarybird is a distinctive, hawk-like bird placed in its own family. Covering about 20 miles a day, it stamps its feet to startle its prey, which includes small mammals, birds, insects, snakes, and lizards. These are chased and seized in the hooked bill. Highly territorial, both members of the pair will run and jump at an intruding bird of their species, holding their wings up and striking out with their feet.

The breeding season begins with nuptial flights, the birds soaring high in the air and calling in a groan or chasing each other about on the ground. A bulky nest of sticks is built in the top of a dense, thorny tree; two or three eggs are laid at intervals of several days and are incubated by the female. She is fed by the male, but also goes off occasionally to feed on her own. At first, the female spends much time near the nestlings, which hatch in 45 days and spend 65 to 80 days in the nest before they fly. Both parents bring food, which except for insects is regurgitated to the young from the adults' crop. Young birds use the nest for a roost long after they leave it.

Peregrine Falcon *(17") family Falconidae*
Falco peregrinus

The hawk-like falcons differ markedly from hawks and eagles in the construction of the syrinx ("voice box") and in their long, pointed wings. The Peregrine, blue-gray with a dark moustache mark and barred below with some streaks on the breast, occurs as a vagrant, migrant, or breeder from northern tundras to the tips of southern continents and on even the most distant oceanic islands. Long famed as the hunting falcon of kings and emirs, it is a master of the air, flying at about 55 miles an hour on a level but achieving as much as a fantastic 275 miles an hour in steep dives. It feeds mainly on birds up to the size of a large duck, killing them with a blow from the feet hitting at high speed or by seizing them in its talons.

Peregrines mate for life. In the breeding season males fly out from selected sites, calling to attract their mates. The pairs fly together, going through remarkable aerial gyrations and screaming. Peregrines build no nest of their own, either scraping a depression in the ground or using the abandoned nest of another large bird; they nest in ledges and sometimes buildings, and in the tundra they may nest on the ground if no cliffs are near. Usually three or four eggs are laid, the season varying geographically; these are incubated mainly by the female, which is very aggressive, driving away other large birds, even eagles, and attacking human intruders as well.

Loss of young to prospective falconers has accentuated a sharp decline in numbers in developed countries, which is probably due to the effects of pesticide poisoning.

On nesting mound

Mallee Fowl *(22") family Megapodiidae*
Leiopoa ocellata

About ten species of the unusual, fowl-like megapodes make their home in the Malaysian, Australasian, and South Pacific island areas. Short-winged and weak-flying, these strong-legged birds often have bare areas on the head. The Mallee Fowl lives in southern Australian scrub woodlands ("mallee") and feeds on buds, flowers, fruits, and seeds, supplemented by insects they chance upon.

Breeding takes up most of the year. Four months may be needed to construct the incubator-like nest, which consists of a deep pit that is dug and filled with all the debris that can be raked into it from the vicinity, then cured by rain-wetting and drying, and covered over with a mound of sandy soil 15 feet in diameter. Starting in September, from five to 33 eggs are laid in the top of the organic layer, in a 1- by 2-foot area, and are deposited at intervals and in numbers that vary with the favorability of the climate. They hatch at intervals until April. The nest is warmed by the heat of decaying organic matter, volcanic soil, soil warmed by hot springs, or the sun. The male literally attends the nest all of that time. He jams his partly opened bill into the mound and thus checks the temperature, which he maintains at about 90° to 95°F. He increases the height of the mound by kicking up more soil, which conserves the internal heat if it is cold outside or further shields the egg chamber if it is hot; he may remove soil in sunny weather (adding sun heat) or to allow excessive internal heat to escape. If a thunderstorm threatens, he runs to the nest to heap a larger mound to shed water, even ignoring humans in his efforts. The young dig their way out after several hours of hatching, scramble under a nearby bush, and are shortly able to go about scratching for food totally without contact with parents.

Great Curassow *(38") family Cracidae*
Crax rubra

Approximately 45 species of guans, curassows, and chachalacas of the tropical Americas comprise this family of pheasant-like birds. Characterized by various structural traits including a hind toe not raised above the others, this family is largely arboreal (tree-dwelling). The Great Curassow ranges from Mexico to northwestern South America in lowland wet forests. Males are largely black with a crest, a white belly, and a globular yellow knob on the base of the bill; females, which vary greatly, are buff or rusty to dark brown, with or without barring, and without the yellow knob, and bear a crest with black and white markings.

Curassows roost and build nests in trees but spend much time on the forest floor eating various fruits. An aggressive whistling note is used toward others of their species and, when habituated to man, toward humans. Turkey-sized males emit booming notes and display in courtship. A small, leafy nest is placed in a tree, and a clutch of two eggs is laid in it. The adult pair attends the nest, females, at least, feigning injury and dragging about to lead an intruder from the nest area before flying away into the trees. Not numerous, curassows are disappearing, killed for food by natives.

Helmeted Guineafowl (22") family Numididae
Numida meleagris

The guineafowls are a small group of seven species found in Africa. Their bare head and neck, very rounded back, and generally spotted dorsal plumage give them a peculiar appearance. Although they fly strongly, they prefer to escape from intruders by running, which they do extremely well. The Helmeted Guineafowl is widespread in the more open areas and brushlands of central and southern Africa and is highly social, congregating in large flocks that walk about the countryside foraging on the ground. Mainly black with white spots, this guineafowl has a yellow-tipped red bill, a reddish, bony casque with an upright or backward projecting prong, and facial wattles that are blue with a red tip. Subjected to domestication since the time of the early Greeks, several varieties—including one that is entirely white—have been developed; the birds are difficult to raise and do not lay many eggs.

Ear-splitting cackling calls by these guineafowl warn all in their vicinity of the presence of danger, and a loud whistling call serves to gather the flock. Nesting pairs scrape a small depression, sometimes lining it with fine grasses, into which the female lays ten to 20 hard-shelled, speckled, yellowish eggs. The female incubates the eggs, but both parents tend the young birds. These guineafowls turn over soil and peck at leaves and debris seeking worms, insects, snails, bulbs, seeds, roots, and other foods; they raid gardens, and sometimes devastate them. As night approaches, they gather at a waterhole to drink, then fly up into a favorite tree to roost.

Black Grouse (20") family Phasianidae
Tetrao tetrix

The grouse are a small subgroup of the pheasant family. They differ from most pheasants and chicken-like birds in lacking spurs on the legs, in having feathers covering the nostrils, and in having the legs and even the toes feathered—or, if not feathered, the toes have comb-like projections. The 18 species of grouse live in North America, Europe, and northern Asia. Some species form pairs, whereas others, such as the Black Grouse, are characterized by the males' promiscuity.

The male Black Grouse is mostly black with brownish wings, a white bar in each wing, an erectile red projection of skin over the eyes, and a black tail the halves of which curve to each side in a broad arc. On a display ground called a "lek," the male displays with plumage fluffed and tail fanned out and held downward, vying with other males for the favors of females attracted to the site. The female is brown barred with white and black, showing only a slightly forked tail. She goes off by herself to scrape a nest in brush at the edge of woodland, lays up to ten eggs, and tends the young for the short period of time required before they are independent. Plant seeds and buds make up much of the diet, but insects are eaten in the spring and summer.

Lady Amherst Pheasant (48") family Phasianidae
Chrysolophus amherstiae

The American quails, partridges, peafowl, chickens, and pheasants comprise ⅞ of the 200 or so species in the Phasianidae. Few of these can compare in beauty with the male Lady Amherst Pheasant, a white-bellied, green-glossed black pheasant of moderate size having a blue patch of facial skin, a red crest, a black and white ruff around the neck, long orange undertail feathers, and a very long, down-curved tail the large central feathers of which are white barred and speckled with black. The smaller female is brownish and barred. As is often the case when the male is brilliantly colored and the female much duller, the female builds the nest, and after laying the six to 12 eggs, incubates them herself and cares for the young thereafter.

This hardy pheasant is found above 7,000 feet in the mountains of eastern Tibet, southwestern China, and adjacent Burma. It feeds on various insects, seeds, leaves, and bamboo shoots, frequenting rocky, brushy areas and open woods. In the winter birds congregate in flocks of up to 30 birds. During courtship, males raise the crest, spread the neck feathers, open the tail overhead, and jump about before the female, making whistling and other noises.

▼ *Male Lady Amherst Pheasant* ▲ *Male Black Grouse displaying* ▼ *Male Black Grouse*

▼ *Female Lady Amherst Pheasant*

Turkey *(34") family Phasianidae*
Meleagris gallopavo

The two species of turkeys are a distinctive group of pheasant-like birds native to North America and northern Middle America. Their bodies are heavy, the feathers are broad and truncate, the tail and wings are wide and rounded, and the bare head and part of the neck have skin projections. Like many pheasants, the males have strong spurs on the back of the legs, used in fighting. Mexican birds were domesticated by Indians as long ago as 600 A.D. After the Spaniards brought them to Europe they became known as Turkeys, because they were confused with similar-appearing guineafowl supposedly introduced into Europe via Turkey.

Found in various woodlands and prairies, Turkeys need trees for roosting at night, but they feed almost entirely on the ground, eating acorns and other nuts, various fruits, grasshoppers and other insects, and a few lizards or crayfish and crabs where they are available; they are able to subsist on buds if other foods fail.

The gobbling males strut and prance in spring, changing the colors of their neck wattles and fanning the tail. Females ready to mate display similarly, and up to six may come to form the "harem" of a single male. They feed together and fly to roost in a tree near the male's strutting ground, but females go off to build the nest and incubate the eggs (up to 18) alone. The young hatch in four weeks and follow the mother about; they are fed insects by her, and she teaches them how to obtain them.

Limpkin *(25") family Aramidae*
Aramus gaurana

A single species, the Limpkin, forms this family, occurring from the southeastern United States to Argentina. Related to the rails, the Limpkin is a streaked brown and white bird with long legs, a long neck and bill, long toes, and rather short wings.

Mainly active at night, this denizen of swamps and marshes feeds on snails and other mollusks, and also on crayfish, other invertebrates, and small vertebrates such as frogs. Its wailing cries are one of the "mysterious" night sounds of southern swamps. The nest is a mass of leaves and plant stems built in dense vegetation beside water, on the ground or in vines or bushes. Both adults incubate the four to seven brown-blotched buff eggs, and tend the hatchlings.

Limpkins may be found roosting in a tree during the day, or one may glimpse them flying over a marsh, long legs dangling in the air as if ready to land momentarily.

Clapper Rail *(12") family Rallidae*
Rallus longirostris

Well over 100 species of rails occur throughout the world except in very cold regions. Although their flight appears weak, they are capable of long, sustained flying and consequently have been able to reach even the most isolated islands in the various oceans. Many island species have lost the power of flight in the course of their evolution, and for that reason such species have been prominent among those birds that have become extinct. Most rails live in marshes or swamps, or about ponds, but some occur in moist forests or damp grasslands. Long-legged and narrow-bodied, they manage to move with ease through the dense reeds and other marsh vegetation.

The Clapper Rail is of moderate size; it is gray-brown with dull markings above, gray and white bars on the abdomen, and a pale throat. With its long bill it grasps and eats various crabs, snails, worms, shellfish, and other animals it encounters in the salt marshes of North and South America, which are its home.

Its loud "krak" calls, in series or as scattered notes, are often the only indication of a skulking bird. The nest is usually hidden beneath a tussock of grass or reeds, of which it is constructed. Up to a dozen eggs are laid; these hatch into downy black young that are able to accompany the adults away from the nest within a short time after hatching.

Sunbittern *(20") family Eurypygidae*
Eurypyga helias

Although related to the cranes, rails, and others of that diverse group, the tropical American Sunbittern is placed in a family of its own. It is peculiar in shape, being rather small-bodied and with long, broad wings, a long tail, a long, pointed bill, moderately long legs, and long, thin toes. The Sunbittern reacts to disturbance by a spectacular wing-spreading display, which confronts an intruder with large chestnut, black, and white spots on a greenish-brown, gray, rufous, and white background. The bird may take mincing steps forward as it displays.

Sunbitterns frequent wet parts of the forest, especially the banks of streams, where they stalk about daintily, seizing frogs, insects, and other small animals. Both members of a pair construct the large nest of sticks in a tree, often beside the water. Two or three eggs are laid and incubated by the parents.

Another distinctive, related group is the Heliornithidae, or sungrebes (also "finfoots"). Three species live in the tropics and somewhat resemble the Sunbittern but differ in having a less variegated plumage pattern, in having lobed toes, and in their swimming habits. The crested Kagu (Rhynochetidae), found only on the island of New Caledonia, may be the closest relative of the Sunbittern. Another peculiar group are the mesites or roatelos (Mesoenatidae or Mesitornithidae), the three species of which are confined to Madagascar.

Sarus Crane *(50") family Gruidae*
Grus antigone

The 14 species of cranes differ structurally and behaviorally from the long-legged storks and herons with which they are sometimes confused. They are social, less dependent on watery areas and trees, and they nest on the ground. Migratory birds, they extend into temperate and even arctic regions. Their long bills are narrow and straight, and their respiratory apparatus is modified for the production of resonant, far-carrying calls. All manner of plants, bulbs, shoots, seeds, grain, snails, frogs, lizards, and snakes are eaten.

The Sarus Crane ranges from Pakistan to the Philippines, and although occurring in the tropics and their fringes, eastern populations migrate as far as Australia. Mainly blue-gray, this species has yellow eyes and a bare area on the throat and upper neck that is red-orange. Displaying pairs point the bill skyward, partly extend and vibrate the wings, and seem to quiver all over as they call loudly.

Nesting occurs when the monsoons begin. The female builds the nest of plant materials. Although territories are large—up to 150 acres—a neighboring pair may visit, display aggressively, and attempt to tear apart the partly constructed nest of a nearby pair. Two or, rarely, three eggs are laid, and both adults incubate them, displaying and calling whenever they change over. One adult remains with the young at all times after hatching. Only one young bird is usually raised, and it remains with the adults for as long as ten months.

Great Bustard (40") family Otididae
Otis tarda

There are 23 species of bustards, heavy-bodied birds of open country, ranging from Africa and Europe to China and Australia. The Great Bustard, one of the large species, occurs in scattered populations across Asia, but hunting has reduced its numbers to the point of its being endangered in Europe.

Barred brown above with a long, grayish neck and white underparts, in flight this bustard shows large white and black areas in the wings. Males are much larger than females and have long, bristly "moustaches." Spectacular in display, the male spreads and turns feathers of the throat, tail, and wings to expose fluffy white feather bases; erecting his moustaches and drooping and shaking his wings (exposing the white and black patches), he grunts and groans.

After mating, the female scrapes a spot in open grassland or cropland, lays two to four eggs, and incubates them for about 26 days until hatching. The young move about with the female soon after they hatch, and she broods and tends them, feeding them insects at first. During much of the year Great Bustards occur in small groups of up to a dozen or so birds. Grain, sprouting plants, clover, peas, grasshoppers and various other insects, spiders, worms, frogs, mice, and even nestling birds form their varied diet.

Incubating eggs

Common Oystercatcher *(17") family Haematopodidae*
Haematopus ostralegus

About six species of oystercatchers occur on the various continents and New Zealand. Several all-black forms have evolved, and it is uncertain whether some or all are distinct species. Most forms are black or brown above and white below, and all have a long, reddish, blade-like bill. The Common Oystercatcher occurs throughout Eurasia, coastal North and South America, and Australasia; below the equator, it migrates to Africa; on the northern continents it flies southward.

Its bill, which is adapted for quick insertion into open shellfish and for cutting through the muscle mass before the shells can be closed, is also used for probing into mud for worms and for cutting barnacles and snails free from rocks. Various crustaceans, shellfish, worms, and crabs make up their diet.

Red-legged, with red eyes and a pied plumage, the oystercatcher is an attractive bird on the mudflats, beaches, and rocks that it frequents. It also lives inland in Europe, but in the New World is strictly confined to the seacoasts. The nest is a scraped area on the upper beach, sometimes lined with a few shells, into which three blotched eggs are deposited. These are well protected by their coloration, for they are difficult to see, as are the mottled young birds.

Avocet (17") family Recurvirostridae
Recurvirostra avosetta

Long, thin legs, a long, delicate bill, a small head, partly webbed toes, and wading habits mark the avocets and stilts, of which about nine species are scattered throughout the world. The four avocets are mainly black and white with an upturned bill. The Avocet of Europe, Asia, and Africa is white, boldly patterned with black on the head, wings, and back. It feeds in shallow ponds and quiet coastal waters, swinging its head from side to side with the opened, upturned bill in the water, thus catching various insects, small fishes, crustaceans, and mollusks.

Social, Avocets nest in colonies in marshes, laying four eggs in a scrape in the sand. The eggs are incubated by both parents, and newly hatched young soon move about following their parents. These dainty birds gather in large flocks late in the summer before migrating southward to warmer climes.

The straight-billed stilts resemble avocets but feed by picking food items from the water. They are even longer legged and more dainty than avocets.

Pratincole (10") family Glareolidae
Glareola pratincola

The Glareolidae is a small family of shorebirds containing the longer-legged Coursers and shorter-legged Pratincoles. Pratincoles somewhat combine swallow-like aerial flycatching habits with plover-like running and feeding on the ground. They have a short, broad bill that opens wide. The Pratincole is found in southern Europe and adjacent Africa, frequenting mud flats and open fields. Fork-tailed, with long wings, it resembles a swallow or tern in flight.

The species is social, nesting in colonies on dry mud flats and migrating in large flocks. Chiefly brown in color, the Pratincole has a white "bib" sharply bordered black, black wings, and a white belly. On the ground it picks up various insects, including grasshoppers, and it takes all types of flying insects as it sails about the air with its mouth open. Three eggs are laid on bare ground and are incubated largely or entirely by the female.

The related Coursers frequent barren regions of Asia, Africa, and Europe, seizing food as they run about. Very fast, they prefer to run from an intruder and fly only when closely pursued.

Killdeer *(8") family Charadriidae*
Charadrius vociferus

About 60 species of plovers and lapwings of this family, characterized by their short neck and short, thin bill enlarged at the tip somewhat like that of a pigeon, occur throughout the world. These "shorebirds" are not confined to the shores, for many occur in open grasslands and barren areas. Northern species are highly migratory; the famous Golden Plover *(Pluvialis dominica)* regularly migrates from Arctic tundras to such southern areas as the Argentine pampas and South Sea islands and back again in the spring, often using a different route.

The Killdeer is a familiar North American species (occurring to northern South America) found in pastures, about croplands, and near ponds and streams. Brown above and white below, it has a white patch before the eyes, two black breast bands, a banded tail, and an orange-brown rump. Its well-camouflaged four eggs are laid on bare ground, often in damp, grassy places. Adults, always quite vocal, protest loudly at any intruder and present a spectacular "broken-winged" display, feigning injury, to draw the intruder from the nest or young. The young move about after hatching, and also are protectively colored and marked. The common call, "kill-dee" is responsible for its name.

Killdeers, like the Golden Plover, migrate southward from more northern areas, but they remain as far north as winter snows will permit and move back north early.

Dunlin (Red-backed Sandpiper) (7") family Scolopacidae
Calidris alpina

About 80 species of sandpipers called by such various names as stints, curlews, godwits, snipe, woodcocks, dowitchers, and turnstones are members of this worldwide family. Except for the snipe, these shorebirds are northern in distribution, many being strictly Arctic in the breeding season. Most are migratory, however, and are widespread wintering birds in southern continents and islands. They tend to be brownish in color and have long, rather slender bills. The Dunlin breeds in northern Canada, Alaska, Siberia, and northern Europe.

In the late spring and summer nesting period, this small sandpiper with a down-curved bill has a rusty back, with a streaked breast and black belly; this plumage gives way to a dull gray and white in late summer. The sexes are alike in color. The grass-lined nest is placed under a grass tussock on a raised area of tundra or, in Europe, moor. Four eggs are laid; the young birds develop quickly and are able to migrate with the adults by late summer. Insects, worms, crustaceans, and small shellfish make up the diet.

Large flocks of Dunlins are found along beaches and mudflats of the coasts and along inland waterways in migration and winter, often in the company of other sandpipers in large flocks. The four species of seed-snipes (Thinocoridae), quail-like small shorebirds of barren lands in South America, and the two Antarctic coastal sheathbills (Chionididae), pure-white pigeon-like birds with a sheath over the inner bill, wattles, and tiny wing spurs, are two other shorebird families.

Silver Gull *(16") family Laridae*
Larus novaehollandiae

Nearly 100 species of gulls and terns make up the worldwide Laridae. Called "seagulls," a general term for the gulls, this subgroup of the family is not oceanic but is generally restricted to coastlines and inland waterways and wet areas. Gulls have webbed feet, a sturdy body, and a hooked, heavy bill compared with terns. The Silver Gull is white with a pale-gray back, some black on the wings, a red bill, red legs and feet, and white eyes bordered by orange or red bare skin. The sexes are alike in color.

Found in Australia and New Zealand, nearby islands, and in southern Africa, this beautiful gull frequents coasts and inland wet areas. It is omnivorous, eating fish, shrimp, and other water invertebrates; frogs; fly larvae in seaweed; some seeds and berries; and eggs and young of other birds. They sometimes force terns and pelicans to drop their food, which they seize. Sewage and rubbish are food sources, and flocks gather behind plows to feed on crickets, grasshoppers, and other insects. Aerial feeding on flying termites has been noted.

A complex series of calls and displays is used in breeding and territorial defense. Nesting is in colonies as it is among most gulls and terns. The nests are constructed of available materials, and lined with grass. Usually, two or three eggs are laid and are incubated by both parents. The incubation period is about 24 days; the young are fed near the nest site for up to four weeks, and they become independent about six weeks later.

Inca Tern (16") family Laridae
Larosterna inca

Almost half of the species in the Laridae are terns, which have straighter, more pointed bills than do gulls; terns dive into the water or pick food from the surface, and they do not usually swim. The Inca Tern of the desert coast of Peru and northern Chile is one of the more distinctive species, gray-black in color with white markings on the wings, a red bill and feet, curving, long "moustache" feathers, and a comb-like flange on the middle toe.

Favoring rocky coasts and islands, Inca Terns are excellent flyers, curving, dropping, or hovering close over the water, then diving for small fish such as anchovies. They have the habit of flying furiously at large birds or other animals, apparently to cause those animals to drop or disgorge food that the terns then seize. Nesting throughout the year, Inca Terns use natural crevices in rocks or old burrows of other birds, or excavate their own nesting burrows among rocks, in which they place their one to two eggs.

Tern-like in appearance, but perhaps more closely related to gulls, are the three species of skimmers or "scissorbills" (Rynchopidae) that ply warmer waters with the longer lower bill inserted into the water to catch fishes and other sea animals. The five jaegers and skuas (Stercorariidae) are gull-like predators that nest in the far north or far south and winter at sea; they eat mice, eggs and young of other birds, and sea animals often obtained from terns and gulls that they harass until food is dropped or disgorged.

Tufted Puffin *(13") family Alcidae*
Lunda cirrhata

The 20 auks, puffins, guillemots, murres, and dovekies are sea-going, diving birds of the "shorebird" assemblage, inhabiting the Arctic and adjacent northern regions. The recently extinct Great Auk *(Pinguinus impennis)*, a huge, flightless auk of the North Atlantic, was responsible for penguins'—their southern counterparts—receiving their name. Auks are heavy-bodied, short-necked birds with legs placed far back on the body, webbed toes, and no hind toe.

The Tufted Puffin is one of the trio of puffins, comical birds with very deep, brightly colored bills, the outer parts of which are shed for the winter, revealing a smaller bill. Summer Tufted Puffins are black with a yellowish tuft of feathers projecting back from the sides of the head, white eyes, red legs and feet, a red ring around the eye, a green-based red bill, and a white face patch. In winter the body is more dully colored, without the white face patch or tufts, the bill is smaller and dull with a reddish tinge, the legs are duller, and the eyes darker.

These birds frequent the waters off the North Pacific coasts and islands, including the Bering Sea and the Aleutian Islands, and range south to Japan and California, wintering offshore in the same region. Breeding colonies are active in late spring on various islands and in rocky coastal areas. The single egg is laid in a crevice or in a burrow dug by the birds. Fishes and invertebrate animals make up the diet.

Pin-tailed Sandgrouse (12") family Pteroclidae
Pterocles alchata

Sandgrouse include 16 species of pigeon-like birds with short feathered legs, long wings, and a long tail. Unlike other birds, sandgrouse and pigeons can dip the bill into water and pump the water into the throat without the need to toss the head back for each swallow.

The Pin-tailed Sandgrouse of southern Europe, the Near East, and North Africa is patterned brown, greenish, black, and white, with well-defined bands of black across the breast. Inhabiting arid and semi-arid country, these birds fly long distances daily to obtain water. Like other sandgrouse, Pin-tailed Sandgrouse are very social, flying and feeding in flocks. Shunning trees, they perch, feed, and nest on the ground. Small seeds, plant shoots, and grain form the diet, and large numbers of tiny stones are swallowed to assist the stomach-like gizzard in digestion of these tough materials.

The two eggs, laid on barren ground, are incubated by the male at night and by the female during the day—the male sustaining the female during the heat of the day by bringing food and water.

Victoria Crested Pigeon (26") family Columbidae
Goura victoria

Usually brightly colored, pigeons and doves numbering about 290 species are found throughout the world except for cold regions. They are characterized by a small bill bearing a fleshy, cap-like enlargement of the base, called a cere, by drinking through a pumping action that does not require repeated dipping and flipping of the bill in water, and by a peculiar fluid, called "pigeon's milk," which is produced in the crop and fed to the young.

The lowlands of northern New Guinea are the home of the beautiful, big Victoria Crowned Pigeon, a ground-foraging species gray-blue in color, with a white wing bar, maroon breast, and large, white-tipped crest. Feeding mainly on fallen fruits, these pigeons fly to the tops of forest trees when disturbed. A single egg is laid in what is (for pigeons) a rather substantial nest of sticks and other plant materials high in the fork of a tree. When not breeding, this red-eyed pigeon moves about the forest in small flocks, flying with a loud whirring of the wings.

Wood Pigeon *(16") family Columbidae*
Columba palumbus

Visitors to Europe familiar with the Domestic Pigeon (or Rock Dove, *Columba livia*) quickly note this large "variety" in parks and countryside. The Wood Pigeon is a closely related species but differs from the Domestic Pigeon in having a white stripe in each wing, a white patch on the sides of the neck, and in lacking a white rump. Wood Pigeons are found across Europe and the Middle East to northern India and may be found courting in Himalayan forests of Nepal as well as in London's parks. Although heavy-bodied, it is agile and can hang upside down if need be to grasp an acorn in its bill. This species feeds on a variety of buds, leaves, grass and other seeds, acorns, beechnuts, fruits, and some insects and snails—it has no aversion to bread tossed to it and looks regal and less hurried than the smaller Domestic Pigeons among which it feeds.

The breeding season is marked by loud, five-noted cooing sounds that serve as a "song." Deeper cooing accompanies displays. With head in and neck puffed out, the male coos as it raises its spread tail, which is closed as the tail reaches its highest point; he then bows to his prospective mate. A display flight involves one or more clapping sounds made by the wings snapped together over the back and concludes in a glide. The two white eggs are laid in an untidy nest built in a tree or bush, or on the ledge of a building. Very young birds are fed "pigeon milk," a secretion produced by the wall of the adults' crop.

Thick-billed Green Pigeon *(10") family Columbidae*
Treron curvirostra

Among the large group of colorful, fruit-eating pigeons called green pigeons is the Thick-billed Green Pigeon of Nepal, eastern India, Burma, and Southeast Asia to Borneo and the Philippines. This fast-flying pigeon is generally gray and green with chestnut under the tail, a purplish back, dark wings bearing yellow stripes, and dark eyes ringed with red or gold surrounded by a bare patch of green or blue skin.

Usually found in small groups, this green pigeon sometimes gathers in large flocks, feeding in the trees on berries and on fruits such as figs, but sometimes birds go down to the ground to eat wild strawberries or to pilfer rice and millet from cultivated fields.

Like other green pigeons, it has an up-down tail-wagging habit, and aggressive individuals bob and bow with open bill. Two white eggs are laid in a fragile platform constructed in a tree, shrub, or bamboo. Well camouflaged by coloration, neither the nest nor the bird is conspicuous in the foliage.

Kea (19") family Psittacidae
Nestor notabilis

Varying in size from less than 4 to more than 36 inches in length, the 320 or so species of parrots form a distinctive and popular family of birds. The hooked, strong "parrot" bill, powerful legs and feet with two toes in front and two behind, nostrils opening in a raised area ("cere"), and a fleshy tongue are some of the traits of these interesting birds. Adept with the bill and feet, parrots seem—and for birds are—highly intelligent. They tend to be long-lived: some of the larger species may live as long as 75 years or more in captivity.

Most parrots are colorful, and generally bring to mind thoughts of dense tropical forests, but the Kea of southern New Zealand inhabits mountains often cloaked with snow. Large and dark green with an elongate hooked bill, Keas have an orange rump and flash yellow and orange in the wings as they fly. They feed on the ground and in trees, eating diverse plants and roots, berries, and insects, and they come to dumps about settlements, as well as feeding on carcasses of animals.

Long thought to harry and kill sheep, Keas have had bounties offered for them, but it seems that only occasionally do they attack injured or snowbound, weakened sheep. Males mate with more than one female and feed the females as the latter incubate the eggs, which are laid in a hollow log or within a rock crevice.

Rainbow Lory or Lorikeet (12") family Psittacidae
Trichoglossus haematodus

An orange bill and orange eyes on a violet-blue head, a red-orange breast, blue belly, orange or yellow nape, green back, and bright red and yellow patches beneath the wings give an indication of why this parrot is called "Rainbow" Lory. Found in the wet forest areas of Australia and New Guinea and on nearby islands, these gaudy birds move about in flocks, sometimes numbering in the hundreds, as they seek blossoming trees.

Lories eat mainly pollen and nectar from tree flowers but also buds, berries, and insects, as well as sometimes descending in numbers on orchards to eat various fruits or on cornfields to eat corn. Their screeching calls and bright coloration attract attention to the flocks as they wheel about the trees. Lories fly through wet, leafy crowns of trees, fluttering there to bathe. Two or three white eggs are laid in a crevice or hollow in a tree. The female does most or all of the incubating, but both parents regurgitate food to the young.

The tongue of this and related species is brush-like, having erectile projections near its tip: these projections were long thought to aid in nectar-feeding, but it is now known that they assist in taking and pressing pollen grains, rendering them suitable for swallowing.

Monk Parakeet (11½") family Psittacidae
Myiopsitta monachus

Native to woodlands and pampas from southern Brazil and Bolivia to central Argentina, the Monk Parakeet is a long-tailed, green parrot with an olive band across the underparts and a gray face and breast. Often found in large numbers about villages and ranches, it is a popular cagebird. This fact is responsible for its being a common escapee, and the species has become established from such escaped birds in Puerto Rico, and recently in the New York City area. Its spread in such areas is a problem, for Monk Parakeets are highly social, occur in large flocks, and eat various fruits and buds of plants as well as insects and seeds. They are considered a pest by farmers in Argentina.

The species is adapted to cool areas, reaching Patagonia in southern South America. Apparently it survives winter snow and cold in the northeastern United States by frequenting bird feeding stations, where sunflower and other seeds are eaten. Unique among parrots, the Monk Parakeet does not nest in a tree cavity or hole in a bank but constructs a bulky nest of sticks in the top of a tree. Several to many pairs share an often huge mass of sticks, each pair having a separate entrance tunnel and chamber within the stick nest. These nests are used for roosting nightly throughout the year.

Scarlet Macaw *(35") family Psittacidae*
Ara macao

One of the largest of the parrots by virtue of its very long, pointed tail, the Scarlet Macaw of tropical forests from Mexico to Brazil is also one of the gaudiest. Adults are bright red with a blue rump, outer tail, and wingtips; a yellow patch in the wings; a bare (unfeathered) white face; and a huge black-and-white bill.

Popular as pets, Scarlet Macaws are disappearing from settled areas of the American tropics. They tend to frequent the edges of forests, openings in the forest, and wooded rivers in open country, feeding in the tops of trees on fruits, nuts, and seeds. The bill of this parrot is strong, and can crack open the hardest nuts; it is also used to enlarge old woodpecker holes or other cavities in trees to form a nesting chamber.

Little is known of their nesting habits in the wild, as they are very wary. Pairs seem to mate for life, and even when these macaws flock together the pairs often are obvious by their perching and flying close to one another. Their feeding sites often are widely scattered, and far from their roosting area. Hence Scarlet Macaws are seen most frequently in flight: either to a feeding area, or to or from the roosting area in the morning or evening.

White-crested Touraco (16") family Musophagidae
Turacus leucolophus

The 18 touracos, or plantain-eaters as they are also called, frequent African forests, where they feed in the canopy on fruits, insects, seeds, buds, and flowers. Brilliantly hued in greens, reds, and even violet, touracos perhaps are distant relatives of the cuckoos, which they resemble in some structural features. They have two toes in front and two behind on each foot, but the outer back toe can be directed frontward or backward.

The White-crested Touraco inhabits forest edges, woods along rivers, and trees in savannas from Nigeria to Uganda, and south to Kenya and Zaire. Its black-and-white crested head, green breast, and violet-blue upperparts render it conspicuous, but like many brightly colored birds of the canopy of tropical forests it is easy to see only when it is moving or crossing open areas.

Usually found in small parties, clambering and running through the foliage, these touracos sometimes gather in large flocks at fruiting trees. A cuckoo-like squealing whistle is their chief call. Two white eggs are laid in a twig nest in the rainy season, often in an isolated tree at the forest edge.

Common Roadrunner (22") family Cuculidae
Geococcyx californianus

A rather long, sturdy bill, a long tail, lax plumage, and feet with two toes in front and two behind characterize the 125 cuckoos that occur on all the major continents. One of the large species is the Common Roadrunner, a comical-looking, brown-streaked, crested denizen of dry grasslands and deserts of southwestern North America that runs about in pursuit of insects, lizards, snakes, and mice. Often cocking its long tail over its back and lifting and lowering it, this cuckoo is well adjusted to an arid climate.

During hot periods when water is not readily attainable, the roadrunner excretes salt from its body on the bill from the nostrils, thus reducing its water requirements. On cold but sunny winter days roadrunners use solar energy to warm up and reduce their food needs by erecting the back feathers to expose normally covered areas of black skin toward the sun. The black skin rapidly absorbs the warmth of the sun and, when sufficiently "charged," the bird depresses the feathers, covering the skin, and goes about its usual activities.

Klaas' Cuckoo (6") family Cuculidae
Chrysococcyx klaas

Many of the cuckoos are nest parasites, that is, they lay their eggs in the nests of other birds, letting the foster parents incubate the eggs and raise the young cuckoos. One of this group is Klaas' Cuckoo, a small green and white species widespread in African forest edges, riverine trees, and savannas. Locally migratory, this cuckoo feeds on caterpillars (a favorite food of cuckoos), other insects, and some fruit. Its breeding season is marked by the monotonous calling of males, a whistled, repetitive "wee-yoo."

Like those of many nest parasites, the eggs of Klaas' Cuckoo are very variable in color, and individual females probably specialize in selecting host species that their own eggs most closely resemble. Usually the eggs are pale in tone, and blotched, resembling those of sunbirds and other small species (some warblers, bulbuls, weavers, flycatchers), but there are instances of pale, whitish, unblotched eggs deposited in the nests of woodpeckers and kingfishers, which lay white eggs. The female cuckoo is secretive when laying and must watch prospective host birds so as to lay its egg synchronously with those of the host. The cuckoo eggs hatch in a relatively short time, giving the young cuckoo an advantage in growth over its nestmates of the host species. This advantage is enhanced by the habit of some cuckoos of tossing out or carrying away one of the host's eggs after (or before) the cuckoo deposits its own egg.

Hoatzin *(25") family Opisthocomidae*
Opisthocomus hoazin

A bizarre, fowl-sized bird shown to be related to cuckoos (Cuculidae), the Hoatzin is a brown-and-buff, white-streaked bird having a mop-like crest and a bare blue area around the eyes. The sole member of its family, it inhabits forested river banks and adjacent, often flooded forests in the Amazon-Orinoco region of South America. Its diet consists of fruits and leaves which are digested in a huge, muscular crop, the evolutionary development of which has resulted in anatomical modification of many surrounding body parts to accommodate it. The bony sternum, to which the flight muscles of the wing attach, is reduced and modified, and the Hoatzin flies weakly, mainly by gliding. Highly social, it often occurs in loose colonies, the birds climbing about trees and harshly calling at any intruder.

The nest is a stick platform built in a tree over water. Two or three brown-marked white eggs are laid and incubated, but nothing is known of the sharing of duties at the nest by the parents. The hatchling birds, almost naked, soon begin climbing from the nest, aided by the presence on each wing of two claws, which are later shed, that are used for clinging to branches. If the young chance to fall into the water, they are able to swim well to a tree, then clamber upward using the toe and the wing claws.

Adult ▲
◀ *Young using wing claws*

▲ Burrowing Owl   Snowy Owls ▲and▼showing variation in markings

Burrowing Owl (8½") family Strigidae
Athene (Speotyto) cunicularia

Owls are hook-billed, usually brown, predatory birds with eyes directed frontward and surrounded by a facial disc of feathers. Most, but by no means all, owls are nocturnal. Except for the ten long-legged species of the barn owl family (Tytonidae), owls represent the Strigidae. The 120 or so species are worldwide in distribution and diverse in habitat; some are specialized for feeding on certain prey such as fishes, but most take any small mammals, birds, lizards, or frogs. The small, brown-and-white mottled and streaked Burrowing Owl is a ground-dwelling species inhabiting grasslands and semi-deserts from western North America and the Florida prairies south to the southern tip of South America. Partly migratory, it has colonized various islands, as in the West Indies.

This owl roosts and nests in burrows of other animals such as prairie dogs and ground squirrels, or it digs its own 1 to 3 yards into the earth. Burrowing Owls are active during the day and may be seen blinking lazily beside their burrow, perhaps bobbing up and down if an intruder approaches too closely. They feed most actively about dusk and dawn, favoring various insects, but they take birds, mice, lizards, and other animals as well. The roundish white eggs usually number five to seven and are placed in the burrow's terminal chamber.

Snowy Owl (22") family Strigidae
Nyctea scandiaca

This great white owl of the Arctic tundra in North America and Eurasia migrates irruptively southward to the United States and to central Europe in years when its food supply fails. This spectacular owl is white with black bars that are narrow or even lacking in many individuals. Lacking the "ear tufts" of most other large owls, the yellow-eyed Snowy Owl is both conspicuous and unmistakable.

It is active during the day as one might expect of an owl that breeds in a place and at a time when there is no night. Perching on a grass clump or fencepost, it seems unafraid and may allow one to approach it closely. It feeds on lemmings and even adult hares in the Arctic, and also takes ptarmigan (grouse, Phasianidae), shorebirds, small ducks, and other birds, as well as some fish.

The nest is on the ground, usually on a hillock or other raised area in the tundra and is lined with feathers and grass. The birds respond in some way to prey they are able to obtain, such that in peak rodent years as many as ten or a dozen eggs are laid, but in poor years only a few eggs are laid or the adults may not attempt nesting at all.

Tawny Frogmouth *(17") family Podargidae*
Podargus strigoides

The dozen or so species of frogmouths form one of the major groups of the largely nocturnal, brown, gray, and black patterned nightjar order. Frogmouths are distributed in the Indonesian-Australasian region and are characterized by a very broad, flat, hook-tipped bill. Instead of flying about, securing insects in the air as do their relatives the nightjars, frogmouths perch low in trees and drop down on insects on the forest floor.

The Australian Tawny Frogmouth is a large species varying greatly in color. By day it perches upright on a branch, looking every bit like a broken stub. At night it perches low and pounces down on roaches, moths, and other large insects, and even mice. The nest is a slight platform of sticks in the fork of a tree. One or two white eggs are laid and incubated by the cryptically colored adults. After hatching, when not attended by an adult, the young assume the typical, upright "frozen" pose of adults.

A related family of Australasian birds, the Aegothelidae or owlet-frogmouths, contains eight small species that nest in hollow trees and combine hawking habits of nightjars with the feeding habits of frogmouths described above.

Distraction display of male ▶

Whip-poor-will (9") family Caprimulgidae
Caprimulgus vociferus

"Caprimulgidae" comes from Latin words for "goat" and "sucker," referring to the supposed habit of these birds' "milking" goats for their food. Among the night flyers of the goatsucker group, the nightjars of this family are the most numerous, the more than 65 species being found on all continents except Antarctica. Large eyes; a mottled and vermiculated brown plumage; long wings and a long tail; a comb-like middle claw on its small feet; and a small bill capable of being opened widely and bordered by bristles that tend to funnel insects toward the mouth are the characteristics of this family.

The Whip-poor-will, so named for its whistled call that is emphasized on the third syllable, is a woodland bird of eastern North America and of the Southwest southward to Honduras. Rarely seen, it perches quietly lengthwise on a branch or on the ground, its colors camouflaging it well. At night it flies about, hawking insects on the wing over forests and open country. In season it may perch and call its "whip-poor-WILL" incessantly, over 1,000 times at a stretch perhaps, then to repeat another long sequence. Calling is most frequent in the evening and in the morning just before dawn.

Two blotched and marked eggs, protectively colored, are laid on the ground in a dark part of the forest or beneath undergrowth. Both adults incubate the eggs and care for the young.

Near nest

The Swift *(6½") family Apodidae*
Apus apus

Among the most aerial of all birds, the 65 or so swifts are aptly named. Shaped like a stubby bullet or cigar with long, sickle-shaped wings, these masters of the air spend the great bulk of their time in flight, rarely perching except to roost, or at the nest. Sometimes confused with swallows, swifts fly faster and often higher in the air, have a shorter tail, and are less graceful and regular in flight movements. Their food is insects caught on the wing.

The Swift is a common European species, gray-black in color, that nests in chimneys, crevices in buildings, and rock cliffs. Squealing flocks of these swifts swirl over many cities and villages. The two or three white eggs are laid in a nest of twigs fastened to the surroundings by hardened saliva.

Asian swifts of the genus *Collocalia* construct nests mainly or entirely of saliva, and nests of some of these species are harvested regularly, the processed gelatinous saliva being used to make "birds' nest" soup commercially.

If inclement weather or other situations arise, the young swifts are able to lower their metabolism and pass up to several days in a torpid state without food.

Costa's Hummingbird (3¼") family Trochilidae
Archilochus (Calypte) costae

Over 300 species of hummingbirds grace the Americas, and they include the smallest species of bird, the Bee Hummingbird, *Mellisuga helenae*. With tiny feet, small legs, very long wings, and usually a long, thin bill, they are distinctive; but their bright colors and flying ability serve to characterize them further. They can hover, and fly vertically and horizontally—backwards as well as forwards. Their bills are adapted for feeding in different groups or kinds of flowers, for many of which they are major pollinators. Most feed mainly on nectar and on the insects attracted to the nectar.

The Costa's is a desert hummingbird of the southwestern United States and adjacent Mexico, making its home in the arroyos among the saguaro and other cacti, among desert trees and shrubs. Males are green above and on the sides, with black wings and a black tail, white on the breast, and with shining iridescent violet on the crown and throat; the throat has elongated violet feathers at the sides that project outward and to the rear. Females lack the violet and have white tips on the tail but so resemble the female Black-chinned Hummingbird *(Archilochus alexandri)* of that region that they are not distinguishable.

The Costa's dainty nest is built in a shrub during the spring, and the female lays two tiny white eggs, incubates them, and rears the young; males meanwhile leave the region for areas to the west and south as the flowering season in the desert comes to an end with the heat of late spring.

Female on nest

Streamertail *(4½", to 10" with tail) family Trochilidae*
Trochilus polytmus

Confined to Jamaica in the West Indies, the Streamertail, or Doctor Bird as it also is called, is abundant there in woods and edges where flowers grow. The spectacular male is bright green with a black cap. It has elongated, frilled outer tail feathers that often bend across one another when the bird is perched; the green and white female has a tail of normal size and shape, lacking the "streamers" of the male. She builds the tiny nest of mosses, lichens, and cobwebs and lays the two white eggs, then tends the young by herself.

Like many hummers, this species can be enticed to feed on a sugar and syrup mix artificially colored (especially red), and placed in a tubular glass container conspicuously placed where the birds are found. This resembles the usual flower-feeding site of hummingbirds, which are the chief pollinators of some flowering plants. The shapes and colors of various flowers have evolved in conjunction with the diversely billed hummingbirds. The sugary diet of hummingbirds, necessary for the energy required to power these feathered dynamos, is supplemented by some insects that the Streamertail pursues in flight or traps with the nectar taken from flowers.

Long-tailed Sylph *(7" male, 3½" female) family Trochilidae*
Aglaiocercus kingi

A very long violet tail marks the male of the Long-tailed Sylph, a hummingbird of the lower mountain forests along the Andes Mountains from Colombia and Venezuela south to Bolivia. The tail is graduated, forming a V, with the outer feathers by far the longest; the female has a much shorter tail.

Little is known of this and of most hummingbirds, but it can be presumed to feed on nectar and insects obtained at flowers. Other than a brief courtship and actual breeding, the male has nothing to do with the nesting effort, as the female builds the nest, lays and incubates the eggs, and raises the young by herself.

Red-faced Mousebird *(14½") family Coliidae*
Colius indicus

The mousebirds or colies are interesting birds of uncertain relationships inhabiting savannas and woodlands of Africa. Crested grayish or brownish birds, the six species have a short bill and long toes and claws, with outer toes that are reversible. They clamber about the foliage in groups, scurrying like mice or hanging like titmice. Highly social, they preen each other and sleep in clusters, sometimes hanging upside down to sleep.

The Red-faced Mousebird is widespread from Zaire and Tanzania to South Africa, climbing and crawling about the bushland trees. Whistling, chirping calls are uttered as these mousebirds fly from tree to tree, seeking fruits such as bananas, oranges, and berries; possibly they take some insects, for captive birds are seen to feed ant pupae to their young.

A stick nest is constructed, lined with leaves, in a dense, thorny tree, and reddish-brown scrawled eggs, two or three in number, are deposited in it. The nest is later used as a roosting platform at night. The young hatch in about 12 days and are naked at first, but they are soon feathered and crawl about the nest site.

Quetzal (13 +24") family Trogonidae
Pharomachrus mocinno

The national bird of Guatemala, giving its name to the currency (the quetzal) of that country and to one of its largest cities (Quetzaltenango), the Quetzal is the largest of the 35 trogons distributed in the tropical regions of the world. Trogons are big-eyed, brightly plumaged, rather stolid birds with soft-textured feathers and feet having two toes forward and two pointing backward.

The male Quetzal is emerald green and crimson, with bristly feathers forming a crest; long, green wing covert plumes; a bright-yellow bill; and greatly elongated green feathers of the upper tail coverts. These last are feathers 2 feet or so in length. The female lacks much of the male's green color, its crest, and its long tail coverts. Males display in flight, the plumes wavering about as the birds call "wak-wak." One behavioral adaptation involving the male's long "tail" can be seen as the bird drops backward off its perch, avoiding the dragging of the tail over rough bark.

Insects, lizards, and fruit are eaten, the fruits being plucked from the tree by the Quetzal in flight. Nesting is in an old woodpecker hole or other hole in a tree. When incubating eggs, the male's tail covert feathers often project from the entrance to the nest cavity. Both sexes share in the incubation of eggs and raising of the young.

Black-capped Kingfisher (11") family Alcedinidae
Halcyon pileata

Husky birds with a large head, small legs, and a strong bill resembling a speartip, the 85 kingfishers and kookaburras are found almost throughout the world. Most species obtain fish by diving into the water in flight, from a hovering position, or from a perch, but some hunt for insects and other small animals in woodlands far from water. All dig a nest in the earth, in a termite nest, or in a rotten tree.

The Black-capped Kingfisher nests in eastern Asia, migrating south to Southeast Asia to spend the winter. A blue back, rusty underparts, black cap, and a large bright-orange bill distinguish this kingfisher, which is one of the strictly water-frequenting species that subsists on fish, although it also takes crabs, frogs, and insects.

The Black-cap pairs excavate burrows a yard or more into a streamside bank, aided by the fused bases of the front toes that, despite the short legs, are used to kick back the earth as the kingfisher digs. At the end of the tunnel is the nesting chamber in which the four or five round, white eggs are laid.

Carmine Bee-eater *(14") family Meropidae*
Merops nubicus

About two dozen brightly colored bee-eaters range from southern Europe and Africa to southern Asia and Australia. A long, thin, pointed bill; long wings; a long tail usually accented by elongated central feathers; short legs; and weak feet characterize these graceful, colorful birds that perch in exposed branches and fly out after passing insects or sail about taking insects in the manner of a swallow. The red, pink, and blue Carmine Bee-eater has especially elongate central tail feathers and is found in two widely separated areas of Africa, across the continent between the Sahara and the Congolese forest and in southern Africa north to Angola. Both populations migrate into the intervening area between them for the non-breeding period.

Found in savanna country, usually near water, the Carmine Bee-eater nests and roosts colonially in holes excavated in riverbanks. For nesting, a 2-foot tunnel is excavated with an enlarged chamber at the end. No material is used for a nest, the three to five white eggs being laid on the bare earth. Perhaps as an adaptation relating to the rough earthen surface, the young have large swellings or pads on the "heel," on which they rest. These bee-eaters are among the birds found near fires, catching insects that are driven to flight.

Dollarbird or Broad-billed Roller *(12") family Coraciidae*
Eurystomus orientalis

Eleven species of rollers, brightly colored, strong-billed birds with long wings, occur from Africa to southern Asia, the Solomon Islands, and Australia. The Dollarbird, so called for its round, "dollar" markings of white in its wings, is deep blue with paler blue wings, a broad red bill, and red legs. From India to China and Australia, Dollarbirds frequent clearings in forests, perching on a conspicuous tree stub or sweeping through the air in broad circles. They seize insects while flying or dart out after them from a perch; they also eat lizards. Much of their feeding takes place in the half-light of dawn and dusk.

Wonderful fliers, Dollarbirds often seem to twist, tumble, or swoop unnecessarily in pursuit of insects, as if indulging in sport. Males display to prospective mates in spectacular flights, zooming about, diving, fluttering and falling, somersaulting, and swerving in front of a female, all the while screaming.

A hollow tree or old woodpecker hole or barbet hole serves as a nest; the three or four white eggs are incubated and the young cared for by both parents.

At nest

Stretching one wing

Southern Ground Hornbill *(41") family Bucerotidae*
Bucorvus leadbeateri

The 45 species of hornbills are found in Africa and southern Asia and are characterized by a large bill usually bearing a casque; bare skin on the face; a long tail; large size; and eyelashes, which are uncommon in birds. Two of the largest species are the ground hornbills of Africa. The Southern Ground Hornbill is a turkey-sized species that waddles about the more open areas of central and southern Africa, seizing grasshoppers and other insects, snails, frogs, lizards, snakes, tortoises, small birds, and mammals. When sufficiently frightened, it flies strongly and loudly, but usually it walks and runs over the ground.

Mainly black in color, its wing tips are white, and the skin around the eyes and on the neck is red in males and bluish with red borders in females. The long bill has a small casque compared with other African and some Asian species. Booming noises resembling the grumbling of a lion are uttered usually in the morning. The nest is a cavity in a stump, log, tree, or boulders, and two white eggs are laid in it.

Unlike most hornbills, the female of which is sealed into the nest by hardened mud plastered over all but a tiny hole and is then fed by the male for ten or 12 weeks until the young are well developed, the female ground hornbill freely enters and leaves the nest. She incubates the eggs, covering them with leaves whenever she goes off to feed. Both adults feed the young, sometimes assisted by young of the previous year.

Chestnut-capped Puffbird (6½") family Bucconidae
Bucco macrodactylus

The puffbirds or Bucconidae number 30 species of big-headed, soft-plumaged, generally brownish birds of the American tropics. Bearing a short, stout bill, hooked at the tip, they are usually seen perched quietly, feathers puffed out. Occasionally they fly out from the perch to seize an insect on the ground or in the air. The nesting habits of most species are little known, but they excavate a chamber in a termite nest or at the end of a tunnel in the ground in which they lay their white eggs.

The Chestnut-capped Puffbird of northern South America is brown with a buff collar, chestnut cap, black-and-white face stripes, and buffy underparts bearing fine black bars. There also are black-and-white breast bands, and spots on the back. The sexes are alike in color.

Possibly related to the puffbirds are the 15 tropical American jacamars, family Galbulidae, birds with somewhat similar but more active habits, with a long, pointed bill, a long tail, and brighter, often metallic colors.

Gaudy Barbet (9") family Capitonidae
Megalaima mystacophanos

Over 70 species of barbets occur in tropical Asia, Africa, and South America, using their stout, pointed bill to seize fruit and occasionally insects in the foliage. Brightly plumaged, barbets have a large head, short neck, short tail, and the yoke-toed foot structure found also in their relatives the woodpeckers. Curiously, although they generally feed very differently from woodpeckers, barbets are most varied and numerous in Africa, which has the fewest species of woodpeckers of the tropical continents.

The Gaudy Barbet of lowland Asian forests is aptly named: mainly green in color, its head is marked with red, yellow, blue, black, and green patches, and, unlike most of its relatives, the female is patterned quite differently. Its series of "tok . . . tok-tok . . ." notes is uttered incessantly for a good part of the year, and even into and through the night. The call is given with the bill shut, and each note is punctuated by a dip or wag of the tail.

Despite its fruit-eating habits and bulky, pointed bill, this barbet (and others) excavates a nest chamber in a rotten tree or stub, there laying its three or four white eggs. Both parents tend the eggs and hatchlings.

Collared Aracari (16") family Ramphastidae
Pteroglossus torquatus

Big-billed, fruit-eating relatives of the barbets, the 36 species of toucans representing this family are comical, brightly colored denizens of tropical American forests. Their long and usually deep bill has serrated edges, and in various species is intricately patterned. The Collared Aracari of Mexico, Colombia, and Venezuela is blackish above with a chestnut collar and a red rump; it is yellow below with a black-and-red band, a red breast mark, and chestnut thighs. Its bill is yellow, black, and ivory, and its orange eyes are surrounded by bare red skin.

Found in small groups, this toucan moves through forests and plantations, daintily plucking fruits with the tip of its bill; it also eats insects, various invertebrates, and probably also baby birds that it chances upon. An old woodpecker hole is used by the group as a "dormitory," which later becomes the nest. The extra birds, probably the young of past years, remain with the nesting pair (although they are forced to sleep elsewhere during the nesting period) and assist in feeding the young and in removing wastes from the nest. Usually there are three white eggs in a clutch, and the hatchling young remain about 44 days in the nest under the care of the parents and helpers.

Rufous Piculet (3½") family Picidae
Sasia abnormis

The 200 or so woodpeckers, piculets, and wrynecks of the family Picidae are distributed throughout the world, mainly in wooded and semi-wooded regions, but they have failed to reach Australasia, the Pacific islands, Antarctica, and Madagascar. Able to excavate their own nest holes in trees, cacti, or earthen banks, most are adapted to feeding on insects on and within the bark of trees. The 20 or so piculets are tiny birds, and they differ from true woodpeckers in lacking the stiffened tail feather shafts, their tails being soft and short.

The Rufous Piculet is mainly rufous in color with a green back; it has a bare, red-violet area around the eyes, and the bill is yellow below and black above. Found in dense undergrowth of tropical forests in Malaysia and Indonesia, Rufous Piculets tap and peck nervously for insects on vines, saplings, and shrubs. They zip rapidly through the dank growth, occasionally pausing momentarily, perched crosswise on a branchlet, to view an intruder; then, with a parting "tic" call, they fly into the forest interior.

The nest is excavated in a tree stub or bamboo shoot, and its entrance is a tiny, neatly rounded hole barely large enough to accommodate its builder.

Andean Flicker *(14") family Picidae*
Colaptes rupicola

Woodpeckers are tree-feeding specialists, and many parts of their body, including the bill; tongue and associated muscles; skull and its musculature; and tail have become modified accordingly. Unusual among woodpeckers is the Andean Flicker, which has forsaken tree-dwelling for a life entirely spent on the ground. It lives above the level of trees in the high "puna" grasslands of the Andes Mountains of South America. There it feeds on insect larvae by probing into the ground, walking (woodpeckers usually *hop*) about the grassy tufts. Nests are excavated in earthen banks or rocky cliff faces, often in small colonies—this being among the most social of woodpeckers. Males are distinguished from females by having some red in their "moustaches," but this can be seen only at close range.

The North American Common Flicker *(Colaptes auratus)*, a widespread, familiar relative of the Andean Flicker, nests in trees or cacti and is thus less adapted for a ground-dwelling existence.

Red-cockaded Woodpecker (7½") family Picidae
Picoides (Dendrocopos) borealis

The most numerous and widespread group of woodpeckers are the so-called pied woodpeckers, including the familiar Eurasian Great Spotted Woodpecker *(Picoides major)* and the common North American Downy Woodpecker *(Picoides pubescens).*

Less known and suffering a severe decrease in numbers is the Red-cockaded Woodpecker of the pine woods of southeastern North America. Barred on the back and streaked below, with a boldly patterned face, this species requires for its nesting a live tree infested with the common red heart fungus. The fungus acts on older pine trees, causing extensive rotting of the heartwood. Such trees are less susceptible to fire than are dead trees, yet they are sufficiently soft to provide easy excavating. Forest management and economy dictate logging of pines well before they are seriously affected by the fungus and, of course, long before they are dead. Hence the rarity of this woodpecker.

Various insects obtained by tapping and probing in the bark form much of this bird's food, but it does eat cherries and some other fruits. A curious habit is the pocking of bark all about the entrance to a nesting or roosting hole; this causes the flow of sap, forming a sticky resinous mess that may serve to deter possible predators such as snakes. Specialized for existence in pinelands, this woodpecker is dependent for its survival on conservation practices that take its requirements into account.

Hornero or Rufous Ovenbird *(8") family Furnariidae*
Furnarius rufus

Generally small, rusty brown, and numerous (215 species), the ovenbirds are a characteristic group of tropical American birds. Various species occupy marshreeds, the forest floor, the forest canopy, the most barren desert areas, grasslands, and the high, cold Andes Mountains. The Hornero of Bolivia and Brazil to Argentina is highly popular and abundant. Rather drab brown with a rusty tail, the Hornero is tame and lives about houses on ranches, in towns, and even in urban centers where parks are found. It feeds on open ground, eating worms and various insects and their larvae.

Its conspicuous nest is an "oven" constructed of mud pellets mixed with rootlets and placed on a fencepost, telegraph pole, a horizontal tree branch, a roof or cornice of a human dwelling, or any structure. The nest is begun long before it is needed and can be built only after rains when mud is available. A foot or more in diameter, it curves inward around a corner so that it is impossible for a human to reach the inner nest chamber. These sturdy structures may last for several years, gracing the landscape.

Noisy, the male and female Hornero frequently engage in a duet, both uttering the loud, ringing song as they face each other, often atop the nest, head stretched out and wings and tail spread and trembling. These choruses also occur after the eggs are laid, when the male and female change over to take turns at incubation.

Red-billed Scythebill (8½") family Furnariidae
Campylorhamphus trochilirostris

One large segment of the Furnariidae, numbering about 46 species, is that containing the woodcreepers or woodhewers. These largely brown, tree-probing species have a long tail with rigid, often projecting shafts, short legs, strong feet and claws, and a variable but sturdy bill.

The Red-billed Scythebill, which ranges from Panama to Brazil and Argentina, has a very long, reddish, tapering, down-curved bill, which is used to probe into the bark and into epiphytic plants growing in trees. Rusty brown in color, this species has streaked and spotted foreparts, including the head. It frequents dense forests where it moves quickly up tree trunks, bracing its body with its long tail, picking up beetle larvae, roaches, scorpions, and diverse insects.

Males sing a series of ringing notes as they feed in the breeding season. The nest is placed in a hole, usually in a decayed tree, and one or two white eggs are laid in it.

Barred Antshrike (6") family Formicariidae
Thamnophilus doliatus

Over 225 strong-legged, hook-tipped bill antshrikes, antbirds, antthrushes, and antwrens ply the forest floors and lower foliage of the American tropical woodlands and forests. The Barred Antshrike of Mexico to Brazil and Bolivia frequents scrublands and forest edges. Males are barred black and white with a short crest, and females are rusty, buff, and white. Pairs sing in duets, uttering a rattling series of notes, tails quivering and crest erect as they call.

The male feeds the female in courtship. Ants, termites, beetles, moths, bees, spiders, and fruits form the food of this species. A moss or grass nest is constructed in the fork of a shrub by both adults. Two spotted white eggs are deposited in the nest and are incubated for two weeks before the naked young hatch. The parents share the incubation and feeding of the nestlings until the latter depart the nest at about 12 days of age, and continue to feed them for a brief period thereafter.

Ocellated Antthrush *(8") family Formicariidae*
Phaenostictus mccleannani

Hordes of army ants move at intervals through various tropical forests. In the New World divers antbirds of the family Formicariidae follow the moving columns of ants, feeding upon them or, more often, upon the insects startled into movement by the ants.

The Ocellated Antthrush of Honduras to Colombia and Ecuador is such a follower, foraging in the undergrowth over the moving ants, eating ants, crickets, roaches, and spiders. Its long tail vibrates up and down as it moves about, ready to dart away into the forest at any disturbance.

Attractive, it has a black-spotted, rufous body, a black throat, and a large blue area of bare skin around each eye, although these colors are not conspicuous in the dense undergrowth. The nesting habits of this shy bird are virtually unknown.

◄ *Male and female near nest*

Peruvian Cock-of-the-Rock *(12") family Cotingidae*
Rupicola peruviana

The cotingas are a group of about 90 varied birds of tropical America. Most are fruit- or insect-eating species of the forest canopy, and hence they are not well known. The Peruvian Cock-of-the-Rock, one of two species of its genus, is a spectacular cotinga. The male is fire-red, with reddish eyes and feet, and a semi-circular, fan-like red crest that extends forward beyond the tip of the bill, often concealing it. There are showy black and white feathers in the wings; the inner wing feathers have wispy, filamentous projections, and the upper tail feathers are long and broad.

Males vie for the favor of females, which are dull and brownish, in elaborate displays performed in arenas that are traditional, i.e., used year after year. A dominant male has several display sites in the arena, and these are kept relatively clear of debris by the bird's display movements. Subservient males are excluded from the active portion of the arena by the dominant birds. Calls, bill-snapping with a head-bobbing motion exhibiting the crest, fanning of the tail, drooping of the wings, jumping and dance-like movements, and postures showing off the various display structures serve to intimidate other males and to attract females.

After mating, females nest, usually semi-socially in a nearby cave, constructing mud nests on the ledges, laying the eggs, and caring for the young without assistance from the males.

Yellow-thighed Manakin (3½") family Pipridae
Pipra mentalis

About 60 small, colorful birds form the tropical American family of the Pipridae. These manakins zip about the forests taking insects from foliage or plucking a berry while in flight. Sometimes they join the various birds following a movement of army ants, seizing insects that are caused to move by the ants. The Yellow-thighed Manakin, which ranges from Mexico to Ecuador, exhibits extreme differences in color between the sexes: the female is greenish and usually has brown eyes, whereas the male has a glowing red head, yellow eyes, a yellow bill, yellow thighs, and a jet-black body.

Males gather in "arenas," each bird having a group of exposed perches in the arena, which usually is an open area in trees high over the ground. Displaying males stretch, showing off their yellow thighs, and swing in that position back and forth, pattering their feet and audibly snapping their wings with each swing. Or they move, stretched, up and down a twig with feet so swiftly moving that they appear to glide. They vary these displays with a back-and-forth flight from perch to perch, calling and snapping the wings. If a female flies to one of the males, he bounces about with seeming abandon. Males spend a large part of the day for several months of the year engaged in these activities.

The female builds a nest, lays the eggs, and raises the young by herself after mating.

Scissor-tailed Flycatcher (13") family Tyrannidae
Tyrannus forficatus

There are more than 350 species of "tyrant" or New World flycatchers occurring from Canada to Chile and Argentina. The bill is usually hooked at the tip, and most species feed on flying insects by sallying forth from perches after them. One of the most attractive species is the Scissor-tail, a dainty, gray and white bird of the dry grasslands of southwestern North America. A wash of pink on the back and under the tail and pinkish-red along its sides and under the wings accentuate the gray tones, contrasting with the long, graduated, white-edged, black streamer tail. Perched on a fence wire, the bird's tail bends in the wind, sometimes over the top of its head. Occasionally the wind may part the crown feathers to show the white-bordered, vivid red patch usually hidden there.

Like the Eastern Kingbird *(Tyrannus tyrannus),* one of its close relatives, the Scissor-tail pursues passing crows, hawks, or other birds that may intrude into its territory. The neatly constructed nest is often lined with cotton and is placed in a bush or tree that may stand alone on the grassland; four to six eggs make up the clutch. The species is rather social, migrating and wintering in flocks.

Vermilion Flycatcher (5") *family Tyrannidae*
Pyrocephalus rubinus

Scrublands and woodland edges from southwestern North America to the Argentine fringes of Patagonia and even the Galapagos Islands far off Ecuador are the home of the Vermilion Flycatcher. The vermilion and brown male, with its brown mask across the eyes, is unmistakable; the female is brown above and streaked on white below, but shows some pinkish or orange on its abdomen.

Vermilion Flycatchers usually perch rather low in a bush or tree and fly out to seize a passing insect. Not exceptionally fast, they maneuver well in a chase, or, hovering, drop upon a grasshopper or other ground insect. Males utter a short song in flight, fluttering high in the air, then zooming downward as the female looks on. Tame, these birds allow close approach before moving away from a human intruder.

Three or four spotted eggs are laid in a nest constructed within a forked branch and are incubated by the female. Both adults feed the young and often raise a second brood. Following the breeding season, Vermilion Flycatchers wander somewhat, even northward. They do not migrate far and return to the breeding area during the late winter in Arizona.

Small-billed Elaenia (6") family Tyrannidae
Elaenia parvirostris

The elaenias are one of many groups of nondescript, tropical American flycatchers. The Small-billed Elaenia is one of the small elaenias, greenish in color, paler below, with wing bars and a white ring around the eye. Found from Bolivia and southern Brazil to Argentina, this elaenia migrates north to northern South America for the period of the southern winter (May to August).

Forests, open woods, and scrublands are the home of this common flycatcher, which usually is seen perched low in a bush, occasionally twitching its tail or sallying out to catch a moth or other insect. Some berries are also eaten when available. A soft song is uttered by males ready to breed. A thick bush is the site of the nest, a cup of grasses, leaves, lichens, and mosses often lined with feathers. Here the two or three red-spotted, whitish eggs are laid, and the young are tended by both parents.

Relatives of these flycatchers placed in their own families are the single species of sharpbill (family Oxyruncidae) and three plantcutters (family Phytotomidae), tropical American species distinct in habits and structure.

White-tipped Plantcutter *(7½") family Phytotomidae*
Phytotoma rutila

The three South American species of plantcutters, relatives of the tyrant flycatchers and cotingas, are semi-social, finch-shaped birds with serrated bills. Males of the White-tipped Plantcutter (of Bolivia to western Argentina) are gray above with white in the tail and wings, and a rufous patch on the crown; the underparts are rufous.

The brown females presumably are attracted by the peculiar creaking sounds that serve as a song. The cone-shaped bill with its toothed edges is used in tearing off pieces of leaves, buds, flowers, and fruits that form its diet. Tending to wander in small flocks when not breeding, these plantcutters often are destructive to orchard trees and other cultivated plants.

Pairs nest in low, often thorny bushes, building an open cup-nest in which the female lays its two to five eggs. These are incubated by the female, although both adults tend the nestling birds.

Superb Lyrebird (37") family Menuridae
Menura superba

The Australasian area is the home of three distinctive families of the great perching bird group. Sharp-billed, short-tailed birds with names like the Rifleman *(Acanthisitta chloris)* and bushwrens form the Acanthisittidae, and two rare scrub-birds, small brown birds with little power of flight and great singing ability, make up the Atrichornithidae.

Related to the scrub-birds are the spectacular lyrebirds, the two species of which are confined to eastern Australia. The Superb Lyrebird is chicken-sized and rather nondescript, but males have a unique tail containing three types of feathers, which in certain positions resembles a lyre. The outermost feathers are broad and curled, enclosing a dozen filamentous, gauze-like feathers and two very long, tapered, and curled plumes totaling 16 feathers, an unusually large number. Females have a long tail, but they barely show signs of the developments found in males.

In the breeding season the male scrapes mounds and clears them at several sites in his territory. Here he displays, first singing elaborate songs, which contain mimicked phrases or whole calls of other birds, mammals, and even mechanical sounds as those of machines; he then spreads his tail over his body. From the front this looks like a silvery, 5-foot-wide veil. The female is attracted to breed, and more than one mates with a single male. Each female then goes off to build its domed nest with no help from the male; she lays two eggs, incubates them, and tends the young.

Crested Lark *(7") family Alaudidae*
Galerida cristata

Larks are generally brownish birds of open country in the Old World. One of the 75 species, the Horned Lark (*Eremophila alpestris,* called Shore Lark in Europe) has reached the Americas in geologically recent time. A rather short, thin, pointed bill, long wings, and an elongate claw on the hind toe characterize the larks, many of which are fine songsters.

The Crested Lark is pale brown above with streaks on its back and breast and a conspicuous crest; the sexes are alike. Found in much of Europe, western Asia, and northern Africa, it frequents dry grasslands, barren sandy areas, and open land about towns. Where not molested, it becomes very tame and may be found in villages among the houses. It walks or runs rapidly on the ground and, shunning trees, uses rocks or buildings as perches. Unlike its relative the Skylark *(Alauda arvensis),* which sings while flying, the male Crested Lark sings his clear, liquid song from such perches.

Both members of a pair construct a nest of grasses and other plants, placing it on the ground in a dry field. Three to six blotched and spotted eggs are laid, then incubated for about 12 days by the female. Both parents feed the young for about ten days at the nest, bringing insects such as small grasshoppers, crickets, and beetles. Often two broods are raised in one year.

During much of the year Crested Larks associate in small groups and feed mainly on grain and on the seeds of grasses of other plants.

Barn Swallow (6") *family Hirundinidae*
Hirundo rustica

The most familiar and widespread of the 80 or so swallows is the Barn Swallow, known in Europe as "the" Swallow. A small but broad bill that opens widely, bordered by bristles; long wings; short legs; and weak feet characterize the swallows, which obtain their insect food on the wing, sweeping back and forth and opening the bill that serves to funnel insects into the mouth. The Barn Swallow has a long, deeply forked tail, is blackish-blue above, has a rusty throat and forehead, white spots in the tail, and cinnamon to white underparts.

At ease on the wing and even drinking water while in flight, this swallow frequents human habitations, nesting inside them or under eaves, under bridges or, occasionally, in caves. The nest is made of mud pellets, gathered wet and mixed with grasses or straw, and formed into a cup that is fastened against or on a ledge; feathers form the lining. Often the nests are clustered, as the swallows are highly social. The three to six colorfully marked white eggs hatch in about two weeks, the female performing all of the incubating. Both adults bring billfulls of small winged insects to the young. Often a second brood is raised after the first have fledged.

The twittering of gracefully circling swallows is one of the pleasing summer sounds. In late summer Barn Swallows congregate in large, even immense flocks before undergoing their extensive migration that takes them as far south as Australia, southern Africa, and Patagonia in South America. In the Argentine pampas during October the throngs of Barn Swallows arrive: one day, none are seen; the next day they are suddenly everywhere, completely outnumbering all of the several local species of swallows.

Scarlet Minivet *(6"–9") family Campephagidae*
Pericrocotus flammeus

The cuckoo-shrikes and minivets comprising this Afro-Asian family of fruit- and insect-eating birds number about 70 species. Varying in color from somber black, gray, and white to bright orange and yellow, these species have a hook at the tip of the bill and a mass of fluffy feathers that detach readily on the lower back. The minivets are a group of colorful foliage gleaners, flitting about the treetops, often hovering in flight to pick an insect from a leaf.

The Scarlet Minivet is blue-black and scarlet, the pattern reminiscent of that of New World orioles *(Icterus),* but the female is more drably attired in yellow, gray, and black. Often they move busily through the treetops in flocks, giving whistled calls at intervals.

Found in India, Ceylon, Southeast Asia, and the Philippines, Scarlet Minivets build a shallow nest of twigs and roots or of mosses, coated with cobwebs and draped with lichens and bark, for effective concealment on a tree branch or rock ledge. The one to three eggs are greenish, blotched with blue and brown, and they and the young birds are tended by both parents.

White-cheeked Bulbul (8") *family Pycnonotidae*
Pycnonotus leucogenys

Over a wide area of northern India and southwestern Asia, the White-cheeked Bulbul represents this family of about 120 thrush-sized, fruit-eating birds with a fluffy plumage and a slender, pointed bill. Mainly brownish-gray, the White-cheeked Bulbul has a short to tall crest, a white-tipped tail, and yellow under its tail. Woods and gardens are its haunts, and there it darts about eating berries or seizing passing insects. Aggressive and vocal, the White-cheek is quick to chase other birds that choose to visit fruit trees in its domain.

A variety of pleasant, whistled notes, such as "peep-a-lo," and visual displays such as erection of the crest, wing flicking, and a pendulum-like swinging of the white-tipped tail in an arc about the fluffily erected yellow under-tail feathers characterize its aggressive behavior. Tame and cocky, this bulbul often enters Indian houses to take table scraps.

Red-backed Shrike *(7") family Laniidae*
Lanius collurio

The shrikes mainly are an Old World family with the greatest number and diversity of species being in Africa. The only American species are the gray Loggerhead Shrike *(Lanius ludovicianus)* of North America and the Northern or Great Gray Shrike *(Lanius excubitor)* of Eurasia and North America. The 65 shrikes are predators on insects and sometimes small birds and mammals, for which habit they have a hooked bill and a strong head and neck. Frequently the prey is impaled upon a thorny tree or barbed wire, where it is torn apart or stored until a later time.

The Red-backed Shrike of Eurasia has the black mask of many shrikes and is gray-headed and gray-rumped with a black tail, rufous wings and back, and buffy underparts. Females differ considerably, being brown above and white below with ventral bars. The males sing a warbled song and mimic other birds in the spring.

A bulky stick nest in a bush receives the five to seven spotted eggs that are incubated by the female. Both adults feed the young, which are soon occupying perches scanning for prey in the manner of adults.

Bohemian Waxwing or Waxwing (7")
family Bombycillidae
Bombycilla garrulus

Three species of waxwings, four American silky flycatchers (Ptilogonatidae, including the Phainopepla, *Phainopepla nitens*, of the arid southwestern United States and Mexico), the Palm Chat of Hispaniola (*Dulus dominicus,* Dulidae), and the Hypocolius (*Hypocolius ampelinus,* Hypocoliidae) of the Middle East, are considered by some closely related, within a single family Bombycillidae. The waxwings are soft-plumaged, tan-brown, crested birds of Eurasia and North America, taking their name from the red, wax-like, modified tips of the inner wing flight feathers.

The Bohemian Waxwing, or Waxwing as it is known in Europe, ranges across Eurasia and the forests of the far Northwest of North America. Neatly garbed in soft cinnamon and tan tones, the Bohemian Waxwing has a black mask below its crest, a black "bib," a yellow-tipped black tail, and black, yellow, and white wings with red "wax" tips on its secondary feathers.

Nesting takes place in June in northern coniferous forests, the nest of evergreen twigs and mosses being placed in a conifer. Four to seven blue-gray eggs are laid and are incubated mainly or entirely by the female, who is fed by her mate. The eggs hatch in two weeks, and the young are fed various insects by both parents. As the young grow, the adults commence feeding them berries and other fruits.

Except when feeding, waxwings are highly social. In certain years, following good supplies of food, great masses of waxwings move southward, thronging to various fruit- and berry-bearing trees. These irruptive migrations carry them into areas not usually visited.

Gray Wagtail (7") family Motacillidae
Motacilla cinerea

The 50 or so species of the Motacillidae, worldwide in distribution, can be divided into two main groups: the widespread, largely streaked brownish pipits (genus *Anthus* and allies); and the more patterned, strictly Old World wagtails (*Motacilla* and allies). All are ground-living species that run about seeking insects, hence they frequent open areas, although a few inhabit streambanks of dense forests.

The Gray Wagtail of Eurasia has a long, white-bordered black tail, rather constantly wagged up and down; the bird is yellow below and gray above, and in the breeding season has a black or blackish-white throat and a gray face patch bordered by two white stripes. It favors the vicinity of small, rushing streams in hilly country during the breeding season, and nests in crevices or ledges in the banks and rocks along the streams. Males have a display flight in which the wings flutter, the tail is spread, and the plumage is fluffed; a special trilling song is given, differing from the musical song given from a perch.

Sometimes an old nest of other birds is the repository of the three to seven eggs, but usually a new nest of mosses, twigs, leaves, and rootlets is constructed, then lined with hair and feathers. The female performs most of the incubating for the two weeks necessary for hatching. Both parents feed the nestlings various insects.

Migrating as far south as Africa and southern Asia, Gray Wagtails are rarely seen away from water. Wintering birds are duller in color, males resemble females, and both sexes lack black in the throat.

Feeding on saguaro fruit

Cactus Wren (7") *family Troglodytidae*
Campylorhynchus brunneicapillus

The true wrens (Troglodytidae) number about 60 species and occur only in the Americas except for one species, the Winter Wren *(Troglodytes troglodytes)*, which extends from North America across Asia to Europe, where it is known simply as "the Wren." Generally brownish, skulking birds, wrens have short wings; a thin, usually somewhat down-curved bill; sturdy legs and feet; and they frequently cock their tail up over the back.

The Cactus Wren of the southwestern United States and Mexico, which frequents scrublands and deserts, is one of the largest species. Brown with a barred tail, a white stripe over the eyes, and dark spots below, its raucous "char-char-char-char" song is one of the characteristic desert sounds.

The rather bulky, globular stick nests are constructed in cacti wherever cacti are available. Nests are used throughout the year for roosting, one bird to a nest, and hence several nests can be found in the territory of a single pair. Young birds are led to such roosting nests by adults, and they construct their own roosting nest when they are about four months old. As many as three or more broods of young are raised yearly. The female is fed by the male as she incubates the eggs. The covered nest affords shade as well as protection from predators. The young remain about three weeks in the nest, being fed by both parents, and are enticed to fly from the nest for the first time by the singing male; adults also withhold food (insects) to encourage the young to leave the nest.

Northern Mockingbird *(9") family Mimidae*
Mimus polyglottos

About 30 species of mockingbirds, thrashers, catbirds, and mockingthrushes make up the Mimidae, a New World family of generally gray or brown birds with a slender bill and a long tail. Gray above and white below with a white-bordered black tail and white-marked black wings, the Northern Mockingbird is a famous mimic and songster, bound in the traditions of the southern United States, where it is common. It has extended its range recently into southern New England and other northern states, and it occurs in the West and into Middle America as well. Usually thought to be a bird of gardens, dense shrubbery, and parks, it takes well to suburban life, but it is also a denizen of desert scrub vegetation in the Southwest.

Always conspicuous and aggressive, mockingbirds sing sporadically throughout the year, often on the wing as they flutter the wings to exhibit the white wing patches. In the spring and summer, males warble, whistle, and sing repetitious mixtures of notes gathered from various sources—other birds' calls and songs, noises of certain machines, etc.—and each male has a unique repertory.

The nest is placed deep within a dense, often thorny tree or bush, and its vicinity is defended with vigor. The mockingbirds are quick to attack any bird that comes too close to the nest, and crows, jays, cats, and other animals are "bombarded" when they are in the area; even humans may be attacked. Two broods of young often are raised in one year.

White-crested Laughingthrush *(12") family Muscicapidae*
Garrulax leucolophus

By far the largest family of birds, the Muscicapidae contains some 1,300 species and is worldwide in distribution, though found primarily in the Old World. All its subgroups are similar, but their interrelationships are uncertain. The 260 or so babblers form one large subgroup. Found in tropical and temperate southern Eurasia, Africa, and Australia, they are characterized by a lax plumage and short wings.

The White-crested Laughingthrush is a striking rufous bird with a crested white head and breast, found in scrub and hill forests of northern India to Southeast Asia. In flocks of up to 40 individuals, these babblers bound about the trees and bushes seeking insects and fruits. Sporadically, one bird will start to call, then the entire group will join in a raucous, cackling, laugh-like calling that rings through the woods. This is accompanied by a frenzied bobbing and wing-flapping. The calling may cease suddenly, only to commence again a moment or two later.

Silver-eared Mesia (7") family Muscicapidae
Leiothrix argentauris

Another and colorful member of the large babbler group is the Silver-eared Mesia of Nepal, India, Southeast Asia, and Indonesia. Frequenting roadsides, scrub, fallen timber, and gardens, this babbler prefers hill and mountain slopes. Males are olive yellowish, green, red, and black, with yellow and red in the wings; red under the tail; a black and gold crown; silvery ear coverts; an orange bill; and pinkish-yellow legs. Females are similar but lack red about the tail.

When not breeding, these sprites move in flocks, the birds clinging tit-like to twigs, searching leaves for insects, and at times flying out after passing insects. Cheep-like notes enable the moving birds to keep together even though feeding out of sight of one another.

Pairs build a cup nest of leaves, twigs, moss, and lichens, lined with fine roots, in a dense bush. Here the several white or bluish eggs, blotched brown, are laid and the young raised.

Hermit Thrush (6½ ") family Muscicapidae
Catharus guttatus

The thrushes form a group of about 300 species of this family, and are worldwide in distribution. The species are diverse but generally share several traits, including the fused scutes or scales at the rear of the legs and the spotted plumage of juveniles. Many species are fine songsters, and several are among the most familiar of birds, as for example the North American Robin *(Turdus migratorius)* and the very different Eurasian species for which the North American Robin was named, "the" Robin *(Erithacus rubecula).*

The Hermit Thrush is a plain brown bird of coniferous and mixed forests in North America; its white underparts have muted spots on the breast, and its rump and tail are rusty. A common species from wet bogs of interior Alaskan forests to the pine barrens of Long Island, its flute-like, quavering song, with rising and falling notes, often uttered in the predawn mist or evening darkness, is a favorite sound of outdoor enthusiasts. Hermit Thrushes are elusive and tend to drift quietly ahead of the intruder so that they often escape detection when not singing. They feed on the ground, seeking various insects and other invertebrates; berries and fruits form a staple food in season.

The nest of grass, roots, and leaves is placed on the ground or close to it, and into it are placed the three or four blue eggs. Although the species may migrate south as far as Guatemala, many individuals winter in the northern United States wherever snow does not accumulate to a great depth.

Blue Rock Thrush *(8") family Muscicapidae*
Monticola solitaria

One of the attractive thrushes of southern Eurasia and Africa is the Blue Rock Thrush, males of which are dark blue with black wings and tail. The female is brown with pale markings. Mountain rock heaps and arid rocky places are its home, and it perches inquisitively on a rock to observe an intruder before bolting out of sight. Various insects form its food, and it must move downslope from colder mountain areas for the winter to insure getting a sufficient diet.

In the breeding season, males sing from rocks or fly upward in a flight display as they pipe their song. A well-constructed nest of fibers and plant materials is placed in a crevice among boulders and is attended by both parents. Occasionally this thrush nests in buildings that bear some resemblance to natural cliffs and rocks.

White-rumped Shama (11") family Muscicapidae
Copsychus malabaricus

The long-tailed White-rumped Shama is a common bird of forest openings in Southeast Asia, north to China, and west to India. It has also been introduced successfully into several of the Hawaiian Islands. Black with a white rump and rusty underparts, its tail makes up more than half its length. The shama perches, often half-cocking and lowering its tail, for a look at an intruder, then darts into the undergrowth. It favors mixed dense forest and open patches, especially near water, and clumps of bamboo. Its place is taken in open country of the same regions by its close relative the Magpie-Robin *(Copsychus saularis),* a very similar, all black-and-white thrush.

One of the finest of Asian songsters, the shama sings a loud, warbled and flute-like, varied song, often from the depths of a thicket and most commonly at dawn and dusk. The male's tail is spread and elevated as it sings. Its loosely constructed nest of grasses, roots, soft plants, and feathers, lined with moss, is placed in some kind of cavity, as a hole in a tree, or within the debris piled at the base of a dense bamboo clump. The three to five spotted green eggs are laid usually between March and June. White-rumped Shamas feed chiefly on the ground, taking worms, various insects, and fruits.

Marsh Warbler (5") family Muscicapidae
Acrocephalus palustris

About 280 species of warblers form the warbler subgroup of this large songbird family, and they are distributed almost throughout the world. Slender billed and tending to be drab in color, the males are usually excellent songsters. The Marsh Warbler of Eurasia is olive-brown above and white below with pinkish legs and a line through the eye. Frequenting dense vegetation near water, such as swamps, it stalks about seeking its insect food.

The male is a fine singer, uttering varied, flute-like notes and whistles, partly mimicking other birds. Night singing is common and sometimes is heard throughout the entire night.

A woven nest of plant stalks and other pliable materials is tied to the stems of low plants, often over water. Three to six blotched eggs are laid in the nest and are incubated for about 12 days from the time of laying of the last or penultimate egg, such that all the young hatch at about the same time. They grow rapidly, thanks to the attention of both parents.

Firecrest *(3¾") family Muscicapidae*
Regulus ignicapillus

The Goldcrest *(Regulus regulus)* of Eurasia, the Golden-crowned Kinglet *(Regulus satrapa)* of North America, the Ruby-crowned Kinglet *(Regulus calendula)* of North America, and the largely European Firecrest are small members of the warbler group of this large family. More southern than the Goldcrest, and less confined to coniferous woods, the Firecrest is olive above, whitish below, with white-marked black wings, a blackish tail, a white line over each eye, and a yellow crown patch bordered on the sides by a black line. In males, the center of the crown patch is orange, whence the name Firecrest.

Nervous, flitting birds, the Firecrests call "zit" as they move about the twiglets and foliage seeking beetles, flies, aphids, other insects and their eggs and larvae, and spiders. Males flutter their wings and erect the brilliant crest in aggressive displays during the pre-breeding period. The high-pitched song of the male is a characteristic woodland sound in the spring.

The female builds the nest of mosses tied with spider webs and bound with feathers, suspending it under the branch of a conifer, while the male perches nearby. Seven to 12 eggs are laid in the nest in May, and a second brood often follows in July. The young hatch after 15 days of incubation and are fed insects and spiders by both parents.

Variegated Blue-wren (4½") family Muscicapidae
Malurus lamberti

About 80 species of Australasian, so-called warblers or wren-warblers compose a distinct assemblage of Muscicapidae, the birds bearing such names as emu-wrens, field-wrens, blue-wrens, and heath-wrens. (Although they cock their tails upward in the manner of wrens, Troglodytidae, they are not close relatives.)

Wet undergrowth in coastal eastern Australia is the home of the Variegated Blue-wren, males of which are patterned rusty, blue, turquoise, purplish, black, and white. Hidden from view most of the time, these birds feed in pairs and small groups, eating various insects. The birds gather at times to display, bobbing about with tails erect and moving animatedly, like mechanical toys.

Dried grass is woven into a ball-shaped nest with an entrance hole near the top; the nest is tucked in the dense foliage of a low bush. Here the somberly colored female deposits her three or four white or pale-red, red-spotted eggs.

Two color phases of species

Paradise Flycatcher *(15") family Muscicapidae*
Terpsiphone viridis

Among the many true flycatchers of this family is a group of long-tailed, attractive paradise flycatchers found from Africa to Japan. The Paradise Flycatcher occupies most of Africa south of the Sahara and is partly migratory. Crested, with a black head and breast, this species has two color phases that are rather distinct in some places but merge in an array of intermediate colors elsewhere. The less common phase, or "morph," is mainly white, and the other is rufous.

Forests, streamside trees, and gardens form the habitat of this elegant, popular bird. Insects of various kinds form its diet and are taken on the wing, the bird sallying out from a favorite perch after its prey. The two or three spotted eggs are laid in a tightly bound nest of bark, fibers, and roots with interwoven cobwebs, camouflaged on the outside by bits of lichen. The nest is usually placed in the fork of a bush or tree, often over water.

Pied Flycatcher (5") family Muscicapidae
Ficedula hypoleuca

Of some 325 species of so-called Old World flycatchers, the Eurasian and North African Pied Flycatcher is a common species of the open woodlands. Black above with a white forehead, a white wing patch, white tail edges, and white underparts, the male closely resembles the male Collared Flycatcher *(Ficedula albicollis)* but lacks the white collar of that species. Females of the two species, brown above and white below, are essentially identical.

The Pied Flycatcher perches conspicuously on branches and flies out after beetles, flies, grasshoppers, and butterflies, and it also takes ants off trees and occasionally worms from the ground; berries are eaten in the fall. The call note is a sharp "pit," the alarm note a "sweet," and males have a bipartite song ending in a trill. The male shows its white breast in display, standing very upright on a perch.

Nests are in holes of various kinds—in walls, trees, nest boxes, or old woodpecker holes—selected by the male but constructed of bark, roots, hair, and feathers by the female. Five to as many as ten pale-blue eggs, sometimes finely spotted, are laid during May and are incubated by the female for 12 or 13 days. The male feeds the female on the nest; both adults feed the young, although the female seems to be the more active.

Red-capped Robin *(4½ ") family Muscicapidae*
Petroica goodenovii

Among the flycatcher members of the large family Muscicapidae are the spritely Australian, so-called robins. Typical of them is the Red-capped Robin of dry Australian woodlands. Males are blackish with white on the wings and tail, white below, and a red cap and breast. Females are brown, duller below, with buff bars in the wings and only a trace of red in the crown. Perching near the ground, they fly to the ground or out into the air to seize insects. The tail is flicked frequently as they perch. Their colors and tame, confiding manner make them a favorite of the Australians.

The nest site is the fork of a branch, and there the pair constructs a nest of shredded bark, moss, and grasses, bound with cobwebs, and lined with feathers or rabbit fur; lichens are woven into the outside, and the dainty structure, less than 3 inches in diameter, is well camouflaged. Two or three spotted bluish or greenish eggs are laid in the nest and are incubated for a dozen or so days. Both parents assist in caring for the young. After breeding is completed the birds become nomadic, wandering about the countryside.

▲ *Male*
Female in nest ▶

Nuthatch (5½") family Sittidae
Sitta europaea

Some 30 species of nuthatches are among the small tree-creeping birds found in Eurasia, Africa, Southeast Asia, and North America. These are rather heavy-set birds with a short neck, short tail, and pointed bill that are able to move about head downward as well as upward on tree surfaces. The Nuthatch is a Eurasian species with a gray-blue back, wings, tail, and crown, a black line through the eye, a white-tipped tail, a white throat, and white to rust-buff underparts.

In addition to feeding on the bark and branches of trees, this species frequently hops about on the ground. It feeds on divers insects, spiders, snails, acorns, hazelnuts, beechnuts, and sunflower seeds at feeders; the nuts and seeds are wedged into crevices in the bark and hammered open with the bill. Males sing several songs; in display they fluff the rusty flank feathers, flutter the wings, spread the tail to exhibit the white spots, and swing the head from side to side. The male also displays with food to the female and feeds her in courtship.

A nest hole is excavated in a tree branch or stem, or a nest box is used; the entry hole is small, and may be made so if initially too large, with mud used as a filler. The six to 13 eggs are laid in a nest of bark and leaves constructed in the hole. The eggs are incubated for two weeks or so by the female, and both parents feed the young.

Other possibly related tree-creeping groups are the six Australian tree-creepers (Climacteridae), the creepers (Certhiidae, six species of which are found in the Northern Hemisphere and Africa), and the two aberrant Philippine creepers (Rhabdornithidae).

Great Tit (5½") family Paridae
Parus major

North America, Eurasia, and Africa are the home of some 65 species of titmice and chickadees, small, chunky birds with soft plumage and strong bills. The Great Tit is a Eurasian and North African species, and is a colorful, common bird of dooryard and park. Yellow-bodied, it has a black head and throat with an extension of black down the center of its breast; there is a white patch on either side of the head, and the wings and tail are blue-gray.

Great Tits are social when not nesting and often join other species in mixed species foraging flocks. A great variety of calls and songs characterize their social behavior. Quick to take advantage of opportunities, Great Tits readily learn to pick food from the hand or lips of a willing human, and in some areas they have learned to pry the tops from freshly delivered milk bottles in order to drink. Many kinds of insects, and especially their larvae, are eaten, as well as spiders, seeds, fruits, and occasionally very small birds of other species.

Nest boxes, holes in walls and trees, and other cavities are used by the pair for nesting, the nest being constructed of mosses and lined with feathers or hair. Five to 12, usually spotted, eggs are laid, and incubated by the female, which is fed by her mate. Both sexes feed the young.

The dozen or so long-tailed tits (Aegithalidae), including the bushtits (genus *Psaltriparus*) of North America probably are not very closely related to the Paridae. Another possibly related group includes nine species of penduline tits (genus *Remiz*), so called because of their long, woven nest, and the American Verdin *(Auriparus flaviceps),* placed together in the Remizidae.

◄ Male
▼ Female feeding young at nest

Mistletoebird (3¾") family Dicaeidae
Dicaeum hirundinaceum

The 55 or so flowerpeckers and pardalotes form this family of Australasian and southern Asian birds that feed on nectar, fruits, and insects. Australia and part of Indonesia are the home of the energetic Mistletoebird. Various berries form its diet, but its chief food is mistletoe-berries. The digestive tract of this bird is simplified, the muscular gizzard or stomach being very reduced; mistletoe-berries pass through the entire digestive system in as little time as 25 minutes. The sticky seeds are undamaged in the passage, and if they are excreted onto a tree branch, they may germinate to spread this parasitic plant.

Mistletoebirds travel long distances from site to site where mistletoe is found. The shiny blue-black, white, and red male helps feed the young, but the brown and white female (which has a red patch under the tail) constructs the intricate, suspended, pear-shaped nest, lays the three white eggs, and incubates them for 12 days until they hatch. The dainty nest is purse-like, with a slit entrance near the top; of plant down bound with cobwebs, the outside of the structure may be coated with lichens, blossoms, or even pieces of caterpillar cases.

Malachite Sunbird *(male 10", female 6")* family Nectariniidae
Nectarinia famosa

From Africa to southern Asia as far east as Australia occur the 115 or so sunbirds of Nectariniidae, in habits the Old World equivalent of the American hummingbirds. Short-legged, with long, thin, curving bills, sunbirds have a partly tubular tongue that can be protruded beyond the tip of the bill; with this they secure the nectar and insects found inside flowers. Males are brightly colored and metallic or iridescent colors are often present.

The Malachite Sunbird of eastern and southern African highlands, an aggressive, large species, feeds on nectar and insects, as well as spiders. Various flowers are sources of food, and some insects are taken by "flycatching." Males, bright green in color with a yellow patch before the wing and an elongate tail, vigorously defend their flower patches and often fight with other Malachite Sunbirds, and even with other birds. The female builds the nest, incubates the eggs, and plays the major role in feeding the young.

Oriental White-eye (4") family Zosteropidae
Zosterops palpebrosa

From Africa through Asia to Japan and Samoa the 90 or so white-eyes of the family Zosteropidae move about through the foliage of trees and shrubs. They are small, generally greenish birds, and most have a well-marked white ring around the eye. White-eyes are social, moving about in flocks, and uttering soft notes that help to maintain contact.

The Oriental White-eye occurs from India to China and Southeast Asia. The sexes are alike in coloring: greenish-yellow, gray, and white with the characteristic white eyering. Insects, nectar, and spiders are eaten, as well as some berries. The birds probe for nectar and insects in various flowers. The nest is a tiny cup of fibers and grasses, bound by cobwebs, and suspended between the forks of a branchlet. Two or three pure-blue eggs are laid.

For small birds white-eyes have shown remarkable ability to cross ocean barriers, some species having reached various islands of the Pacific and Indian Oceans.

Red Wattlebird *(14") family Meliphagidae*
Anthochaera carunculata

About 170 slender-billed birds with brush-tipped tongues that feed partly on nectar make up the family of honeyeaters or Meliphagidae, occurring from Australia through New Guinea to many Pacific islands, including New Zealand and even Hawaii.

The large, streaked Red Wattlebird of Australia bears a 1-inch red wattle on its cheeks and has a yellow patch under the tail. Partly migratory, highly social, and pugnacious, this noisy bird gathers in numbers at flowering eucalyptus and other trees, probing the flowers for nectar and insects. It also eats various orchard fruits and is unprotected in some areas as a pest; in fact, it once was hunted as a game bird. It may cause some damage to cultivated flowers in gardens, breaking them to get the nectar.

Yellow-tufted Honeyeater (7½") family Meliphagidae
Meliphaga melanops

Another of the honeyeaters, the Yellow-tufted Honeyeater, is found in wet woods, forest edges, and gardens of southeastern Australia, but it occurs only in widely scattered colonies. It is mainly olive-yellow with a black facial mask and black bill, and a yellow throat and yellow feather tuft on the ear coverts. An active bird, it frequents the outer foliage of trees, probing under the bark for insects, occasionally darting out in flight after an insect, taking nectar from flowers, and eating fruits. Predators such as owls are mobbed by calling Yellow-tufted Honeyeaters.

A shredded bark and grass nest, bound with cobwebs and lined with soft animal or plant materials, is placed or even suspended in a low fork of a tree or shrub during the spring and summer. Two or three buff eggs bearing spots are deposited in the nest and incubated, and the young tended until they are independent.

Greater Racket-tailed Drongo (13" + tail to 17")
family Dicruridae
Dicrurus paradisaeus

Some 20 species of drongos, family Dicruridae, inhabit Africa and southern Asia as far east as some Pacific islands. Drongos are inveterate flycatchers, sallying forth from perches after nearby insects. They are aggressive, often attacking bigger birds and driving them away.

The Greater Racket-tailed Drongo is all black, like most drongos; the black shows a metallic sheen. Its forked tail has two greatly elongated middle feathers, without vanes except at the tip, where they form a "racket" (40 percent of adults have broken or abnormal rackets).

From India and Ceylon to Java pairs of this drongo frequent forest clearings. Ringing, even bell-like calls are uttered, and the drongos mimic many other birds that they hear. Intruders are challenged by calls and watched closely by the drongos that peer from beneath their bedraggled black crest. The three or four blotched eggs are laid in a grass, fiber, and leaf nest placed in the fork of a tree.

Black-faced Woodswallow (7½") family Artamidae
Artamus cinereus

Southern Asia to Australia is the home of the woodswallows, ten species of which form the family Artamidae. These are stout-bodied birds with long wings, short legs, and stout bill. Mostly gray or brown, they fly about, swallow-like, catching insects on the wing.

The Black-faced Woodswallow is gray above and white below, with a black tail and face mask. Found in open woods of the interior of Australia, it swirls over the countryside in groups or perches on conspicuous perches from which it occasionally flies out on a foraging flight. Ravens or other potential predators that fly nearby sometimes are mobbed by the woodswallows.

A loose nest of twigs or roots is built in dead shrubs, on fences, on television poles, or in sheds. Three or four pinkish eggs bearing reddish-brown spots are laid in the nest and are incubated for 16 days. The young birds are tended by the adults for two and a half weeks before they leave the nest.

Satin Bower Bird *(12") family Ptilonorhynchidae*
Ptilonorhynchus violaceus

The bower birds number 17 species and are found in New Guinea and Australia. Stocky and rather short-tailed, they show a number of unusual habits. The Satin Bower Bird of eastern Australia shows a strong sexual difference in color, males being a velvety black with a violet sheen, females gray and green with barring.

In the breeding period, the male builds a stick platform with two stick walls that curve together to form a chamber. This is constructed in a 4- by 2-foot arena that is kept clear of all vegetation, and the walls are oriented so that the morning sun does not shine into the chamber. The bower and the arena are decorated with objects (mainly blue) of all descriptions—flowers, berries, feathers, glass, plastic, etc. Not content with this, the male macerates vegetable materials and uses them to brush (paint!) the bower walls, discoloring them a yellowish or other color. The male is near the bower most of the day, protecting the items from other males. The arrival of a female triggers intense displaying (the male prances, gallops, bounds about the bower with tail up) and calling (croaking, chattering, whistling, mimicking humans, cats, and other birds), culminating in copulation in the bower. A male may mate with two or three females in a season, the latter going off to nest without the male.

▲ *Female inspecting bower after male has prepared it* ▶

Greater Bird of Paradise *(18") family Paradisaeidae*
Paradisaea apoda

About 42 of the most ornate bird species form this Australian and New Guinea family. A strong bill that may curve somewhat and strong but short legs are structural features of the group, along with the marvelous array of skin structures, modified feathers, and varied colors responsible for their name. Southern New Guinea forests are the home of the Greater Bird of Paradise, males of which are maroon, bright green, and golden yellow with masses of long, lacy flank feathers and two very elongated, wire-like central tail feathers. Females lack ornate plumes and are plain brown in color.

A dozen to 20 males congregate in certain open display trees during the breeding season. One or a few dominant males in full adult plumage maintain choice display sites in the center of the tree. Fantastic wing-spreading and vibrating displays, with the "wires" of the tail held up over the bird and the flank feathers erected in a golden swirl, mark the charges and other interactions of the males. When a female arrives, the males "freeze" into a full display position, and she walks among them before making her choice. Dominant males do most of the mating with visiting females, which then go off to build a nest, lay two eggs, and incubate the eggs and tend the young without help from the male.

Common Raven *(26") family Corvidae*
Corvus corax

100 species of the widely distributed Corvidae include two major groups of crows and jays (these include ravens, rooks, choughs, and magpies). The ravens are large members of the generally all-black crow group. The Common Raven is found in the Northern Hemisphere south to Nicaragua, central Africa, India, and Japan: it has the distinction of being the most northerly occurring bird and also is larger in body size than any other of the thousands of perching birds (order Passeriformes).

Long-lived, wary, intelligent, and adaptable, the Common Raven is a master flyer, soaring great distances on updrafts of air. Seacoasts and mountain crags, deserts and Arctic tundra are its domain; although it sometimes lives near humans, it prefers wild areas. The raven's diet is varied, including carcasses on highways; carrion of all sorts; weak or injured animals; newborn mammals; mice; lemmings; birds of various sizes and their eggs; dead fish; snakes; frogs; snails; clams; various insects; fruits; and seeds including grains.

Common Ravens seem to mate for life. The male and female construct a lined nest of sticks on rock cliffs or in a large tree. The three to seven eggs are incubated for three weeks essentially by the female, who receives food from her mate. Both adults feed the young for their six-week nestling period and thereafter until they become independent. The species is resident throughout the year, and its croaking call is a familiar sound in regions it inhabits.

Magpie-Jay *(24" including 14" tail) family Corvidae*
Calocitta formosa

One of the largest and most handsome of the jays, the Magpie-Jay occurs in Mexico and Central America, favoring arid and semi-arid scrublands. Longer than a crow, over half its length is in its white-edged blue tail. It has a blue body with white underparts, a black face with a blue patch, a black or white throat, and a wispy crest, but the elongated tail dominates its appearance. An intruder quickly gains sight of this jay as it sails in through the trees, tail streaming behind, to utter a raucous challenge—and, incidentally, to warn the local wildlife. They are usually encountered in groups of up to half a dozen birds, perhaps representing long-lasting family parties.

Nesting takes place over a great part of the year. A rather bulky stick nest is meticulously lined with fine rootlets and other plant materials, and three to seven eggs are laid. The female incubates the eggs, being fed at the nest by the adult male and often by one or more attendant "helper" birds that presumably are the previous year's offspring. The young are fed fruits and various insects.

Magpie-Jays are omnivorous, taking even the eggs and young of smaller birds and joining vultures and ravens in cleaning up carcasses of animals killed by automobiles along the highways.

Yellow-billed Oxpecker (8½") family Sturnidae
Buphagus africanus

Old World areas from Europe and Africa to the islands of the Pacific are the home of some 105 starlings, representing the Sturnidae. These are varicolored, short-tailed, strong-legged birds, many of them highly adaptable, conspicuous species of open country. Most familiar among them is the Common Starling *(Sturnus vulgaris),* an aggressive Eurasian bird associated with man in urban and rural settings; this species has been introduced in the Americas and elsewhere to the detriment of native bird species.

Unusual among starlings, and birds, is the Yellow-billed Oxpecker, an orange-eyed, brown and yellowish bird with a sturdy, broad-based bill that spends its daylight hours climbing over the backs of African domestic and wild mammals in search of the ticks on which it feeds. Hanging like a woodpecker or tit to the sides of such animals as buffaloes, the oxpeckers are quick to call in alarm when intruders are seen, thus warning their hosts.

The birds retire in flocks to marsh reeds for the night. Oxpecker nests are mats of grass and hair or feathers placed in a cavity in a tree, in rocks, or in buildings.

Paradise Whydah or Widowbird (15") family Ploceidae
Vidua (Steganura) paradisea

The weaverbirds or weaver finches number about 155 species found in Africa and Eurasia, with several species introduced widely elsewhere. A short, conical bill, short legs, and a stocky body mark these small birds. Much of Africa is the home of the Paradise Whydah, or Paradise Widowbird as it is also called. These seed-eaters are unusual in habits and appearance, males being black, white, and buff with an elongate black tail having broad, curved central feathers, and females being streaked, brown-and-white birds with a short tail.

Breeding males first gather in flocks, but then separate into distinct territories, over which they fly in slow display flight, the tail floating out behind them. Females are attracted to the displaying males; after mating, they seek the nests of certain finches, mainly Melba Finches *(Pytilia melba),* in which to deposit their eggs. The eggs are incubated and the young raised by these foster parents. Assisting in the deception is the close resemblance in pattern of the mouth of young widowbirds to the black-spotted, gaping mouth of the Melba Finch young as they beg for food.

▲ Oxpeckers on back of rhinoceros ▼ Close-up of Yellow-billed Oxpecker

◄ Male Paradise Whydah

145

House (English) Sparrow (6") family Ploceidae
Passer domesticus

Among the most familiar of birds, and dweller with man in villages, towns, and even the centers of the largest cities, the House Sparrow is native to Europe, North Africa, and northern and central Asia. Transported to New York City in 1852, it rapidly extended its range to include most of North America, and it can be seen as well on Argentine ranches, in Australian and South African cities, and on many islands throughout the world, thanks to introduction by man.

Largely brown above and grayish-white below, the sexes differ in pattern: males have a gray crown, chestnut hindcrown, white cheeks, and a black throat; females are streaked brown above and have no throat patch or chestnut and gray on the crown. Their plumage frequently shows the signs of urban pollution—soot, grime, and grease.

Although widespread, House Sparrows are more or less restricted to the vicinity of human habitation, rarely occurring in natural habitats. Pairs nest, often repetitively, in all sorts of crevices in and near buildings—under roof tiles, in lighting fixtures, in traffic lights, under air conditioners—actually, any place they can enter. In some areas they nest in trees as their ancestors presumably did, constructing a large, circular mass of sticks with the entrance at one side. They also build their nests within the massive nests of storks and large hawks. Bird nest boxes are also used. Four to seven eggs are laid and incubated for two weeks before hatching. Insects form part of the diet, but seeds, grain, other plant materials, and bread and other items tossed to them by humans are also consumed.

Gouldian Finch (5") *family Estrildidae*
Poephila gouldiae

About 110 species of small to very small, usually brightly colored finches comprise this family, and are found in grasslands, marshes, savannas, and woodland edges of the Old World tropics from Africa to Australia. Very social, they feed on or near the ground, build domed nests of grasses, and have squeaky, weak voices. Many are commonly kept cagebirds, and a favorite among these is the Gouldian Finch of the grassland scrub and woodland edges of northern Australia. This colorful finch is violet, yellow, and white below, and green above with a blue rump and blue around the head. Its head usually is black, but genetic variation occurs, and one bird in four has a red cap and face with a black throat; much rarer is a yellow-capped variant. The black tail has elongated, pointed, central tail feathers.

Unlike most related grassfinches or waxbills (as members of the family are called), the Gouldian Finch forgoes a domed nest and seeks cavities in termite mounds or in trees in which it places its loosely constructed nest. The eggs number four to eight, and both parents share in the incubation of eggs and feeding of the young. In favorable years, two or even three broods of young are raised in a single season. Large amounts of grass seed and other seeds are eaten by this finch, but in the breeding period most of the diet consists of ants, termites, and other insects.

Evening Grosbeak (7½") family Fringillidae
Coccothraustes (Hesperiphona) vespertina

The 115 or so finches of this family have a conical bill well adapted for seed eating; other anatomical features separate them from other sparrow-like groups. Found throughout Asia, Africa, Europe, and the Americas, these finches tend to be erratic in their migrations. Northern species erupt southwards particularly in years when the northern seed crops fail. Some, often colorful, species are attracted to winter feeding trays placed out for them by humans, and one of these is the Evening Grosbeak of North America.

Males have a dusky black head and throat, a yellow forehead, yellow underparts and back, a black tail, and black wings with a white patch. Females are grayish, showing yellow traces. The bill of this species is massive.

Evening Grosbeaks inhabit coniferous forests of the far north and the mountains of western North America south to southern Mexico. They migrate irregularly southward, sometimes appearing in great numbers, other times being absent from an area. In the present century they have been going south and east for the winter in ever greater numbers: first reported in the New York area in the early 1900's, they now appear in at least low numbers yearly, and throngs often gather at bird-feeding stations.

Pairs construct a nest of twigs and bark within a conifer, usually near its top. The female lays three or four speckled, greenish eggs, and she incubates them until they hatch.

Yellow-throated Vireo (5") *family Vireonidae*
Vireo flavifrons

About 40 species of small, generally gray or greenish birds with a finely notched tip of the bill make up the Vireonidae, a strictly American family. Largely insectivorous, they methodically pick their food from the bases of leaves and in the foliage of trees. The Yellow-throated Vireo inhabits eastern North America, favoring large deciduous trees in open forests or in parks. Mainly greenish, mixed with gray, its wings are black with two white bars, the tail black, the abdomen white, and the breast, throat, and a "spectacle" around the eyes bright yellow. Its slow, hoarse but loud song, "three-eight . . ., three-eight . . ., three-chew" is a characteristic woodland sound of the early summer and is uttered high in the trees.

Moths, various beetles, caterpillars, and other insects are plucked from the foliage by this vireo. The nest is intricately woven of grasses and fine bark fragments, held together by spider "silk" taken from webs; the outside of the nest is covered with lichens attached by spider webbing. The structure is fastened to the fork of a twig so that it is suspended and actually sways in the wind. Three to five blotched eggs are laid within it and incubated by both parents for the two weeks necessary for hatching.

Yellow-throated Vireos leave in September for Central America, where they winter.

Akiapolaau (5¾") family Drepanididae
Hemignathus wilsoni

One of the highlights of avian evolution, the Hawaiian honeycreepers are a group of about 15 diversely adapted birds that have proliferated in the Hawaiian islands from a single ancient ancestor that managed to reach there. In the absence of competitors, various species evolved, differing greatly in bill structure and feeding habits. There are stout-billed "finch"-like forms; thin-billed birds; and long-billed nectar feeders, all small and some colorful. Unfortunately, the coming of modern man, with his agricultural practices, his introduction of competing and predatory pests, and disease vectors, has been responsible for extinction of several of these fascinating birds, and the rarity of most of those remaining. The extant species are largely montane forest birds, difficult to find; indeed a distinctive species forming a genus of its own managed to escape detection until 1974.

The Akiapolaau is a unique, bark-creeping, green bird with a long, curved upper bill, and a heavy, short, straight lower bill. This species forages by using its lower bill, woodpeckerlike, to probe, tap, and pry at the bark and into crevices; it then grasps insects so exposed with upper and lower bill, or it may clasp a piece of bark with its bill and toss it aside, then feed. The Akiapolaau has a tube-shaped tongue like its nectar-feeding relatives, but does not eat nectar.

Blackburnian Warbler *(5") family Parulidae*
Dendroica fusca

A distinctive American group of largely insect-eating or nectar-feeding birds, the wood-warblers, so called to distinguish them from unrelated Old World birds known as warblers, range from the Arctic fringes to southern South America and number about 120 species. Most are colorful birds of the forest foliage (at least the males are, as is so often the case when females do much or all of the incubating of eggs), but some live in marshes or on the ground or frequent desert shrubs. Several species are at home in the northern evergreen forests, but they show their tropical origin by migrating far to the south for the winter.

The Blackburnian Warbler is colorfully patterned, black and white in the male, and brown and white in the female with a throat and face of bright orange in the male and of muted orange in the female. It breeds in the largely evergreen forests of mountains in the eastern United States and in eastern Canada and spends the winter in southern Central America and northern South America. Moving almost impatiently, it flits about foliage of taller trees of all kinds in its migration through the eastern United States.

Once known as the Hemlock Warbler, its nest is often placed in a hemlock tree. The song of the male is high-pitched and is one of those that we humans, as we age, tend to lose our ability to hear.

Western Tanager (7") family Emberizidae
Piranga ludoviciana

About 530 species of tanagers, cardinal-grosbeaks, and buntings (including some of the "sparrows"), formerly considered as representing distinct families, are now placed in the Emberizidae. All but one small group of buntings are exclusively American in distribution, ranging throughout the two American continents. The tanager subgroup is found mainly in the tropics, but several species range into North America, including the colorful Western Tanager. The mountains and valleys of western North America, south barely to Mexico, are its summer home; it winters south to Costa Rica.

The male in summer is bright yellow with a black back, wings, and tail, white wing patches, and an orange-red head; in fall and winter he is duller, without the red, thus more closely resembling the green and yellow female. A rather stout, pointed bill bearing a notch along each side serves to seize caterpillars and other insects from the foliage that is searched diligently as well as in eating fruits.

The male sings a warbling song, maintaining its territory as the female prepares a loose nest of twigs, bark, and other materials, lays the three or four spotted, bluish eggs, and incubates them for two weeks. Both parents then feed the nestling tanagers, which develop and soon resemble the mother in color and in size.

Paradise Tanager (6½") family Emberizidae
Tangara chilensis

Among the many tropical American tanagers that add color to the forests are several feathered gems of the genus *Tangara*. Fruit- and insect-eating species that move about in flocks containing various species, the "tangaras" frequent the canopy of the forest. From northern South America south to Bolivia, the gaudy Paradise Tanager forages in a deliberate manner, picking berries, other fruits, grasshoppers, beetles, flies, and spiders from the foliage.

The sexes are alike, green on the head and face, satiny black on the back with red and yellow about the rump, and turquoise blue and black below. The black wings bear purplish on the edges and turquoise at the bend of the wing.

Little is known of the habits of this and of many tropical forest species, many of which stand to become endangered or even extinct as the vast forests are destroyed.

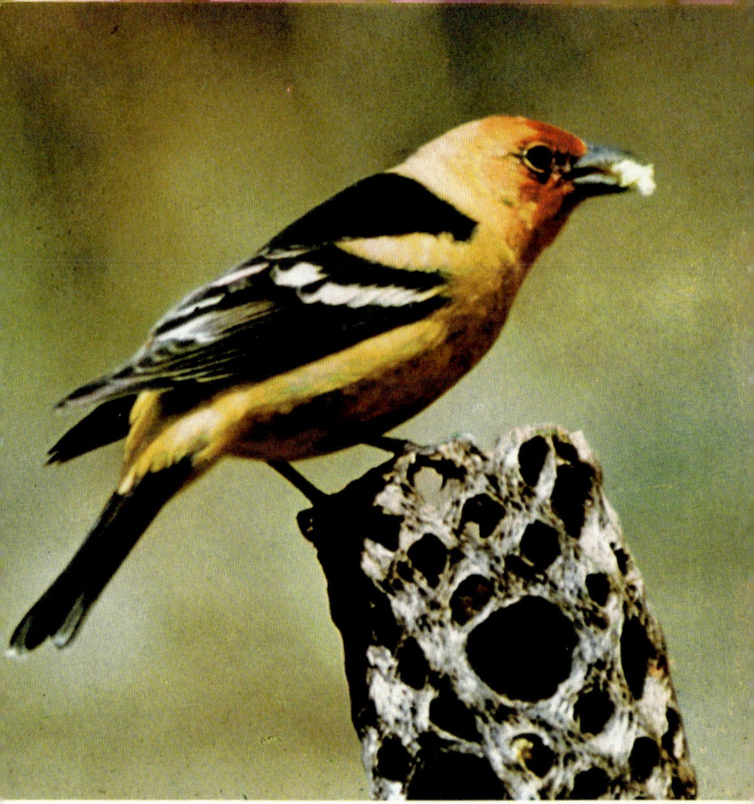

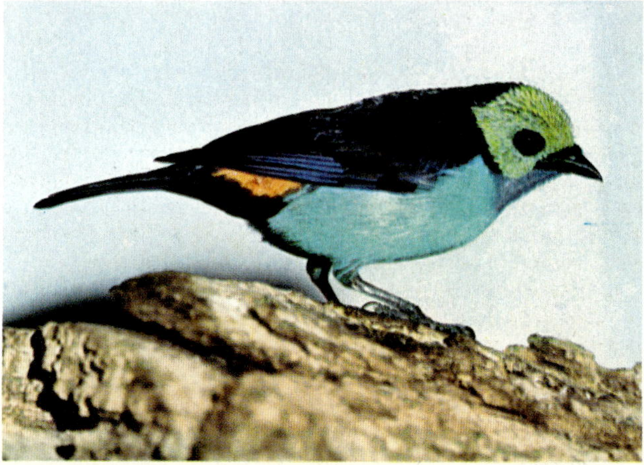

Pyrrhuloxia (8") *family Emberizidae*
Cardinalis sinuata

A large group of finch-billed, colorful birds in this family includes the popular Cardinal *(Cardinalis cardinalis)* of North America and its less well known, but striking, relative of deserts in southwestern North America, the Pyrrhuloxia. The latter has a red crest, and a heavy, curved, stout bill reminiscent of the bill of a parrot. Male Pyrrhuloxias are gray-bodied with red around the eyes and bill to the breast, as well as on the wings, tail, and legs. Females are brownish with less red.

Favoring the streamside, more dense vegetation of the desert, this species also is adapting well to suburban living in Arizona and Texas. Its cheerful whistling song complements its colors, adding to its attractiveness. Like many finch-billed species, it has a mixed diet, eating caterpillars and other insects and their larvae when it can, but also feeding on fruits of cactus and other plants and on seeds of grasses and of some acacia-like trees.

The female selects a site for a nest, usually in a thorny bush or within a dense thicket, builds the nest of various plant materials, lays three to four spotted eggs, and incubates them. Her mate sings nearby and assists in the raising of the young.

Painted Bunting (6") family Emberizidae
Passerina ciris

One of the major groups of the Emberizidae, the cardinal-grosbeak group, includes among its colorful members several species of the genus *Passerina,* called buntings, that are particularly pleasingly colored. The well-named Painted Bunting perhaps is the most colorful of them. The sexes differ markedly, the female being entire yellow-green with no patterning; the male has blackish-purple wings and tail, a purplish-red rump, yellow-green back, bright-red underparts, a violet-blue head, and a red ring about its dark eyes. Although strikingly colored, the males often skulk in dense shrubbery, as do females, throughout the range of the species in the southern United States and northern Mexico. Near habitation, however, it often can be seen on lawns.

Painted Buntings subsist on various beetles and other insects taken on the ground and on grass seeds and other seeds that make up most of their diet in winter. The nest is a neat cup made of grasses, twigs, and leaves and is hidden within a dense bush. Three to five speckled eggs are laid in it late in the spring. Both sexes care for the young. Flitting its wings and spreading its feathers, the male displays and sings in establishing and maintaining its territory through the spring and summer.

Grasshopper Sparrow (4½") family Emberizidae
Ammodramus savannarum

Among the generally brownish sparrows and buntings of this large family, the Grasshopper Sparrow is one of the least conspicuous, yet is widespread and abundant. Vast areas of such regions as the North American Great Plains support dense, continuous populations of this species, which occur from Canada to northern South America in grasslands. Yet the casual observer may not be aware of the presence of Grasshopper Sparrows, short-tailed, brown-streaked mites that stay close to the ground or on it, and utter a wheezy, weak song that passes for the sound of an insect to the uninitiated human.

Three to five speckled eggs are laid in a nest constructed of grasses, often arched over the top to conceal it, on the ground in dry grassland. If one chances to find the nest by stepping near it, thus flushing the incubating adult, one may witness a distraction display, the bird weakly hopping about, wings distended as if the bird were injured, until the intruder is led far enough from the nest, whereupon the sparrow suddenly recovers and flies off.

Various insects, appropriately including grasshoppers, form the bulk of its diet, but seeds of grasses and weeds are also eaten.

Spot-breasted Oriole (8") family Icteridae
Icterus pectoralis

Nearly 90 species of American orioles, oropendolas, troupials, "blackbirds," grackles, meadowlarks, cowbirds, and the Bobolink *(Dolichonyx oryzivorus)* form the American family Icteridae, members of which range from Alaska to Tierra del Fuego. Often patterned with black and yellow (or orange or red), most species have a rather long, pointed bill that can be used in gaping as a means of food finding—the bill is inserted into plants or the bark of trees and opened to expose insects or other foods. The species are varied in diet and in habitat (which runs the gamut from wet tropical forests to marshes, arid grasslands, and deserts).

The Spot-breasted Oriole is a brilliant orange bird with black tail, wings, back and throat patch, and spots on the breast, as well as white wing patches. Found from Mexico to Costa Rica, usually in arid scrub vegetation, it has been accidentally and successfully introduced into the area about Miami. Renowned singers, males are recognized by their long, rather complex, clear whistled songs; the females, which look like the males, whistle simpler songs.

The nest of this oriole is an intricately woven, bag-like structure of plant fibers and leaves suspended from the tip of a branch, usually of a tall tree, where it swings about in the breeze. Despite its complexity and size—it is often 18 inches or more in length—it is woven in as few as five days.

Index

A

akiapolaau, 150
albatross, 26
antbird, 102
antshrike, 14, 102
antthrush, 102, 103
antwren, 102, 103
aracari, 96
Archaeopteryx, 7
auk, 14, 67
avocet, 61

B

babbler, 120, 121
barbet, 92, 95, 96
bee-eater, 91
bird of paradise, 7, 141
blackbird, 157
blue-wren, 127
boatswainbird, bosunbird, 29
bobolink, 157
booby, 30, 34
bower bird, 7, 140
bulbul, 78, 114
bunting, 152, 155, 156
bushtit, 132
bushwrens, 110
bustard, 59

C

cardinal, 154
cardinal-grosbeak, 152, 155
cassowary, 21
catbird, 119
chachalaca, 50
chickadee, 132
chicken, 52
chough, 142
cock-of-the-rock, 5, 104
coly, 88
condor, 43
cormorant, 29, 30, 31, 32
cotinga, 104, 109
courser, 62
cowbird, 157
crane, 57, 58
creeper, 131
crow, 106, 119, 142
cuckoo, 76, 77, 78, 79
cuckoo-shrike, 113

curassow, 50
curlew, 64

D

darter, 32
diver, 23
doctor bird, 86
dollarbird, 92
dove, 69, 70
dovekie, 67
dowitcher, 64
drongo, 138
duck, 9, 35, 36, 37, 38, 48, 81
dunlin, 64

E

eagle, 9, 45, 48
egret, 39
elaenia, 108
emu, 19, 21
emu-wren, 127

F

falcon, 48
field-wren, 127
finch, 144, 147, 148, 150, 154
finfoot, 57
firecrest, 126
flamingo, 38
flicker, 98
flowerpecker, 133
flycatcher, 106, 107, 108, 109, 128, 129, 130
fowl, mallee, 49
frigatebird, 34
frogmouth, 82

G

gannet, 30
goatsucker, 83
godwit, 64
goldcrest, 126
goose, 35
goshawk, 46
grackle, 157
grassfinch, 147
grebe, 9, 24
grosbeak, 9, 148
grouse, 52, 53, 81
guan, 50
guillemot, 67

guineafowl, 51, 54
gull, 60, 65

H

hammerhead, 40
hawk, 9, 44, 45, 47, 48, 106, 146
heath-wren, 127
helldiver, 24
heron, 9, 39, 40, 41, 58
hoatzin, 79
honeycreeper, Hawaiian, 150
honeyeater, 136, 137
hornbill, 93
hornero, 100
hummer, hummingbird, 9, 85, 86, 87, 134
hypocolius, 116

I

ibis, 41

J

jacamar, 94
jaeger, 66
jay, 119, 142, 143

K

kagu, 57
kea, 72
killdeer, 63
kingbird, 106
kingfisher, 78, 90
kinglet, 126
kite, 45
kiwi, 22
kookaburra, 90

L

lammergeyer, 45
lapwing, 62
lark, 111
laughingthrush, 120
limpkin, 55
loon, 23
lorikeet, lory, 73
lyrebird, 7, 110

M

macaw, 75
mallard, 36
mallee fowl, 49

158

magpie, 142
magpie-jay, 143
magpie-robin, 124
manakin, 105
man-o'-war bird, 34
meadowlark, 157
megapode, 49
merganser, 37
mesia, 121
mesites, 57
minivet, 113
mistletoebird, 133
mockingbird, 119
mocking-thrush, 119
mousebird, 88
murre, 67

N

nightjar, 82, 83
nuthatch, 131

O

oriole, 113, 157
oropendola, 157
osprey, 44
ostrich, 15, 19, 20, 21
ovenbird, 100
owl, 9, 80, 81
owlet-frogmouth, 82
oxpecker, 144, 145
oystercatcher, 60

P

palm chat, 116
parakeet, 74
pardalote, 133
parrot, 72, 73, 74, 75
partridge, 52
peafowl, 52
pelican, 9, 29, 30, 31, 33, 34
penguin, 9, 25, 67
petrel, 28
phainopepla, 116
pheasant, 9, 50, 52, 53, 54
Philippine creeper, 131
piculet, 97
pigeon, 8, 14, 62, 64, 68, 69, 70, 71
pipit, 117
plantain-eater, 76
plantcutter, 108, 109
plover, 62
potoo, 83

pratincole, 62
ptarmigan, 81
puffbird, 94
puffin, 67
pyrrhuloxia, 154

Q

quail, 52, 64
quetzal, 89

R

rail, 55, 56, 57
raven, 139, 142, 143
rhea, 19, 20, 21
rifleman, 110
roadrunner, 77
roatelo, 57
robin, 12, 13, 28, 122, 130
rock thrush, 123
roller, 92
rook, 142

S

sandgrouse, 68
sandpiper, 64
scissorbill, 66
screamer, 35
scrub-bird, 110
scythebill, 101
seagull, 65
secretarybird, 15, 47
seedsnipe, 64
shama, 124
sharpbill, 108
shearwater, 27
sheathbill, 64
shoebill, 40
shorebird, 81
shrike, 115
silky flycatcher, 116
skimmer, 66
skua, 66
skylark, 111
smew, 37
snakebird, 32
snipe, 64
sparrow, 146, 148, 152, 156
spoonbill, 41
starling, 144
stilt, 61
stint, 64
stork, 40, 42, 58, 146
storm petrel, 28

streamertail, 86
sunbird, 78, 134
sunbittern, 57
sungrebe, 57
swallow, 9, 62, 84, 91, 112, 139
swan, 35
swift, 9, 84
sylph, 87

T

tanager, 5, 152
tangara, 152
tern, 62, 65, 66
thrasher, 119
thrush, 7, 114, 122, 123
tinamou, 18
tit, titmouse, 88, 121, 132, 144
toucan, 96
touraco, 76
tree-creeper, 131
trogon, 89
tropicbird, 29
turkey, 54, 93
turnstone, 64

V

verdin, 132
vireo, 149
vulture, 42, 43, 44, 45, 143

W

wagtail, 117
warbler, 78, 125, 127, 151
waterfowl, 35
wattlebird, 136
waxbill, 147
waxwing, 116
weaverbird, 7, 78, 144
whip-poor-will, 83
white-eye, 135
whydah, 144, 145
widowbird, 144
woodcock, 64
woodcreeper, 101
woodhewer, 101
woodpecker, 14, 78, 89, 92, 95, 97, 98, 99, 144, 150
woodswallow, 139
wood-warbler, 7, 151
wren, 7, 110, 118, 127
wren-warbler, 127
wryneck, 97

159

Special Offer

If you enjoyed this book
and would like to have our catalog
of over 1,400 other Bantam titles,
including other books in this series, just
send your name and address
and 25c (to help defray
postage and handling costs)
to: Catalog Department, Bantam Books, Inc.,
414 East Golf Rd., Des Plaines, Ill. 60016.

Dr. Lester L. Short is a Curator in the Ornithology Department of the American Museum of Natural History, and an Adjunct Professor on the Graduate Faculty of the City University of New York. A graduate of Cornell University, he is a Fellow of the American Ornithologists' Union and American Association for the Advancement of Science, as well as Secretary of the Pan-American Section of the International Council for Bird Preservation. Dr. Short's researches have involved field studies on six continents, resulting in more than 100 scientific publications.